To my dear Easter family –

JEAN DARNALL

Heaven...
Here I Come!

A DOWN-TO-EARTH, DEATH-TO-LIFE STORY

Jean Darnall — Lu 4:18

Oct 14, 1998

Ventura, Ca.

WinePress Publishing
MUKILTEO, WA 98275

Contents

FOREWORD

If it's necessary, permit me to introduce Jean Darnall to you. (But there are few places this is needed, because this book is written by one of the most traveled, most loved and most respected women in the twentieth-century Church.)

It was with great delight I learned that *Heaven, Here I Come* was about to be reprinted for new and even broader distribution. Then, an added delight: I was asked to write a few words of introduction—a foreword, with my own privilege of remarking on this remarkable person.

There are so many ways to approach describing Jean Darnall and her ministry; each of which providing a distinct and beautiful facet of this lady whose life has touched millions and altered the destiny of at least tens of thousands.

- She is a gracious yet dynamic evangelist who communicates the gospel of Jesus Christ both with fervor as well as with winsome gentleness.
- She is a capable teacher of systematic, biblical truth; for years ministering beside her beloved husband, Elmer, as a professor at London's Christian Life Bible

College, as well as in pastorates they have served in the United States, England and Australia.
- She is a clear thinking and interesting writer, with books to her credit, as well as innumerable articles and published sermons.
- She is a devoted wife (she and Elmer have been married fifty-five years), a loving mother (both of whose children are involved in vital Christian ministry), and a doting grandmother (the most fulfilling of her many vocations!).

All these things are verifiably true and could be illustrated with factual incidents. But I want to tell my favorite "Jean" story; one that might be titled by the words, "I Had Been Miraculously Healed, and I Didn't Even Know Who Had Prayed for Me!"

It was over forty years ago, and Jean Darnall was already well established as a trusted, well-recognized evangelist, with an especially sensitive graciousness in the ministry of healing.

She had come to Angelus Temple, the church adjacent to LIFE Bible College, where I was studying for the ministry. Only days before, I had been seriously injured while involved in athletic competition—now, only able to move with great pain, and generally confined to my dormitory. Without detailing the story, it's essence is in what happened after I was virtually carried into the service where Jean was praying for the sick—right at the end of the meeting while she was ministering to the last person in the line of those coming for prayer.

I had not been in the service, but many of my dormitory friends had, and seeing the manifestly miraculous work of God in progress, they had rushed to my room to find me. As they assisted me from my room, to the church and then to the platform, I didn't know anything about the service of the evening, the message that had been preached, or even the name of the woman about to pray for me. But I immediately knew one thing:

The instant she laid hands on me, along with the elders of the church, I was healed! And as I walked off the platform—aglow with joy and relieved of the intense pain in my body—I knew I needed to keep walking briskly, in the supernatural strength my body had received. So I walked directly up the aisle of the church and out the front door.

Try and picture it, please: I had been almost carried in—just in time for prayer; and immediately strode out into the night! It would have been ingracious, except the crowd was so large, no one noticed. But the memory is still almost as hilarious as it certainly is precious. "Walk in for instant healing, walk out touched by God" might have been a slogan for the event, at least as I experienced it! Still, as I remember it—even with the hint of humor in my sudden appearance and departure—there is nothing to be taken lightly about the reality of that miracle moment, nor of the righteous and anointed way that healing ministry was administrated that night.

Peculiarly I forgot about the *person* God used (though I was later told Jean's name that evening). This is probably because what Jean seems to always most impress people with is not herself, but with Jesus! So it was not until several years later that Anna and I met her and I recalled that pivotal moment in my own experience, years before, and actually came to know the person the Holy Spirit used so mightily to touch my life with the power of the Lord Jesus Christ.

Today, Jean Darnall is not only a dear friend of our family but a beloved, frequent guest minister to our congregation at The Church On The Way. We regard her as a "mother in Israel," so to speak: a spiritual forebear, whose life and witness have not only contributed greatly in shaping our own lives, but whose influence had done much to shape the course of the Church in different parts of the world over the past half-century.

So, please, meet Jean Darnall . . . and please read on. As you do, I think you'll sense you are once again in touch with a Book-of-Acts-type person, whose almost matchless uniqueness in ministry is always matched with a very godly and gracious humility.

JACK W. HAYFORD, pastor
The Church On The Way
Van Nuys, California
October, 1997

CHAPTER ONE

THE TEXT
ON THE WALL

'We'll have to get her into the hospital for surgery,' Dr. Brady, our family physician, told my mother. 'Maybe if we remove one kidney, Mrs. Murphy, the other one will rally. I can't promise anything, but we can try.'

My fever began to climb on Monday. Infection spread through my body. My ears abscessed. The signals were all flaring for a major attack of kidney poisoning. Pain gripped my back. On Tuesday my temperature bounced from 102° to 104°F.

All day Wednesday words that the woman evangelist had said on the previous Sunday night throbbed through my feverish mind again and again. 'On Wednesday night there will be prayer for the sick. Jesus Christ is the same yesterday, and today, and forever.' She had pointed to a text painted on the wall behind the pulpit— 'Jesus Christ, the same yesterday, and today, and forever.' I could see the text now, wobbly and wavy like water flowing through my burning brain. The words rang high and clear. 'On Wednesday night there will be prayer for the sick. Jesus Christ is the same yesterday, and today, and forever.'

Mother came into the bedroom to relieve the nurse. 'Mother, if you take me to the "angel lady",' for the blonde lady preacher seemed that to me, 'I believe she can do something for me,' I whispered. 'Let's try,' I pleaded.

Tears glistened in my mother's eyes. 'I believe she can, too,' she said.

My mother never went to church. She was much too busy. She owned and managed a restaurant in Toledo, Ohio where her southern fried chicken and home-made pies attracted a good trade. A hard-working Irish woman, she had a heart as generous and good as her meals. Everyone trusted and admired Mrs. Murphy. It came as a surprise when she began to ask her customers and employees, 'Can you tell me where I can find a church like the old-fashioned Methodist one, a church where I can get saved?'

'Saved, Mrs. Murphy? Why you're twice as good as most people who go to church. Why do you want to get religious?'

A death in her family had started it all. Her eldest brother, a coal miner in West Virginia, had frozen to death as he was working on the tipple of the mine. He had been a mean, cruel man and my mother had suffered horribly because of him. It was with little grief, except for the family, that my mother attended the funeral in the mountains of West Virginia and stood by the grave in a bleak blizzard. 'If there is a hell,' my mother thought, 'John has gone to it.'

Suddenly, closer that the cold wind that blew through the mountain pines, she heard a voice say, 'There is a hell and you're going there, too!' She glanced quickly around at the others who stood shivering in the swirling snow. None of them had spoken to her. Who was it? It seemed she had heard that voice before.

She began to recall a childhood incident. She remembered the excitement around the family farm when word came through others who lived in the West Virginia hills that a Methodist woman preacher was on her way with a team of horses and a wagon. She needed a field to pitch her tent for some special services. My grandfather's cow pasture was the chosen site. This preacher was like a one-woman church. She played the pump organ with two feet and one hand, leading songs with the other. Then she'd take an offering and preach. When she called penitents to the 'mourners' bench' my mother was among the miners and farmers who knelt there. She was only nine years old, but she never forgot how the sunshine coming through the canvas warmed her back and head as she prayed.

'It seemed like God was smiling on me,' she told me later. 'I've never felt so close to him as I did then. Maybe if I could find a church like that here in Toledo, I'd feel peace in my soul again,' she reasoned.

My mother was a troubled woman, in spite of her good business and reputation. Money could not buy the thing our family needed the most—health. My father, disabled from the first World War, was in and out of government hospitals getting treatment for his lungs which had been damaged by chlorine gas. My kidneys were fast deteriorating from the effects of ptomaine poisoning I'd had when an infant. The doctors had already told my mother that one kidney was no longer functioning and the other was not likely to hold out much longer. Mother's cheerfulness and courage could not ward off the growing concern she had for both of us. 'I've taught you how to live, but not how to die,' she once said to me.

So she had started to shop for a church. Every Saturday she selected one from the newspaper's church directory. She would attend one in the morning and another in the evening. I'd ask her when she returned, 'Did that one suit you?'

'No,' she'd say with disappointment. 'They looked at my hat rather than my heart. Why they didn't even say "hello", much less ask about my soul'.

'What are you looking for?' I asked.

'I'm looking for a church where I'll hear the gospel preached like that Methodist woman preached it. I want to go to a mourners' bench and feel close to God again.'

'Look, Mother, you're out of date. There aren't any churches like that any more'. I informed her. I felt like I was a bit of an expert on church. Although Mother had been too busy to go to church and Dad was always too sick, they had both insisted that I should go. So they sent me to the one nearest at hand. It had to be in walking distance. The first one was the Methodist Church. I had a Sunday school teacher there who had a missionary heart. No matter what the lesson was, Mrs. Keyes would end up with a missionary story. I became acquainted with David Livingstone, Jonathan Goforth, Hudson Taylor and other missionary heroes. A desire to please the Lord began to grow in my heart. A question came that insisted upon an answer: 'How may I please God?'

When I asked Mrs. Keyes, she exclaimed, 'Oh that is a very important question! You must go to the pastor and ask him, Jean,

So I put my query to the pastor. It didn't seem difficult for him to answer. 'Oh, that's simple,' he said. 'To please God one should become a Methodist!'

After brief instruction, I was baptised and became a Methodist.

The next church I went to, when we moved to another neighborhood was the Baptist church. Something inside me was not satisfied with the simple answer I had received in the Methodist church. So I asked my question again. The youth leader listened and sent me to the pastor.

'What has been your religious experience, Jean?' the Baptist pastor asked.

'I'm a baptised member of the Methodist church.' He opened his 'Baptist Bible' and showed me that I ought to be baptised by immersion. 'That will please God,' he assured me.

I seemed to have missed the significance of it all, for I found I went down a dry sinner and came up a wet sinner! I felt somehow that what I had done had hardly made any difference to God.

We moved again and I started to attend the Lutheran church. This time I went directly to the pastor with my question, 'How may I please God?' I explained my two baptisms.

'Well, Jean, I don't believe you need to be baptised again,' he said with a twinkle in his eye. 'You're at the age now when I think it would be good for your to be confirmed.'

I studied my catechism fervently and with a great deal of solemnity I received my confirmation. My natural inclinations towards religion had put me in good standing with the church.

Later I began to go to the Presbyterian church. My reasons were purely social. By that time I had decided that no one could really please God. Besides, it seemed that it didn't particularly matter to him whether we tried or not. My Presbyterian pastor knew a great deal about Sigmund Freud and much of what he had to say from the pulpit agreed with my atheistic science teachers. Also, I liked the boys that went to this church and I loved to dance. Those who attended Sunday morning services were entitled to dancing lessons at half price in the church basement each Wednesday afternoon.

So, by the age of fifteen, I had become quite an expert on churches, and it was with the voice of experience that I told my mother, 'Churches don't have mourners' benches any more. People are not likely to go up front and kneel to say they're sorry for their sins nowadays—not in this modern age.'

Mother wasn't easily discouraged. The Voice wouldn't let her forget that there was a hell and she was going there. She couldn't shake off the chill of death.

The one who came to show my mother the way to find God didn't look at all like a messenger sent by heaven. She was a tottering old lady who came to the back door of our restaurant seeking a dishwashing job. As the frail little figure struggled with the stacks of dishes in the hot kitchen, she almost fainted. Seeing her swaying, Mother caught her and promptly decided to take her home with her. 'Come home with me and be our grandma,' she invited. She soon became a welcome member of our family, and we always knew where she was because she was so unsteady and was always dropping things. There was a clatter and a bang all day long, so I nicknamed her 'Bumbang'.

It was not long before she got involved with Mrs. Murphy's search for a place to get saved. One day she came toddling out of her bedroom with a magazine in her hand.

'You know, Mrs. Murphy, I think I've found the church you're looking for.' She held up a rather shabby, aged magazine. On the front was the face of a smiling, auburn-haired woman who was holding a white Bible. Above her head the banner read 'Foursquare Bridal Call'. The date on the magazine was 1922—it was fifteen years old.

'Looks like they've got a woman preacher connected with this somehow,' Bumbang said.

'Where did you find this?' Mother asked, taking the magazine.

'My brother who lived in Boston, Massachusetts, died recently.' Mother looked up, quickly remembering her own brother's recent death.

'He's been writing to me for years about salvation,' Bumbang continued. 'I've never paid much attention to his letters—they were just pages of the Bible verses. Anyway, he died. Since I'm his only relative, friends of his sent all his personal belonging to me in a big trunk. I found this magazine at the bottom of it.'

Mother sat down on the edge of my bed where I lay propped up with pillows. My legs were aching and swollen with rheumatism. Leafing through the magazine, she read, 'What is the Foursquare Gospel?' I looked over the pages with her and read the paragraph headings, 'Jesus Christ the Saviour', 'Jesus Christ the Healer', 'Jesus Christ the Baptiser with the Holy Ghost', and 'Jesus Christ the Coming King'. I leaned back, thinking about those words, 'Jesus Christ the Healer'. When Mother had finished reading, she looked up and said, 'This comes from Los Angeles, California. I wonder if there is a church like that here'?

'It's Saturday, look in the paper,' I said.

Opening the *Toledo Blade* to the religious news page, she scanned the list of churches. 'Nothing here by that name,' she said. 'Wait, look at this!' A display advertisement stood boldly in the middle of the page. 'Announcing the opening of the Foursquare Gospel Church in Toledo. Old-fashioned revival services every night.' There was the address of the place, the times the services began, and a friendly 'Everyone welcome!' In each lower corner, not to waste any space, were the words 'Jesus Saves' and 'Jesus Heals'.

'Well, that's just about as corny as it can be!' I exclaimed. 'Imagine "old-fashioned revival services!" What kind of people do they expect to attract with copy like that?'

'We're going!' was Mother's reply.

Mother told some of the employees at the restaurant about the advertisement and several wanted to come, so we had a full taxi the Sunday evening we started out to the new Foursquare Church in Toledo, Ohio. Even I, in spite of my legs hurting, was bundled into a taxi. Dad, grumbling all the way, came along, too. He had hoped that, since our car was in for repairs, he'd be able to talk us out of it, but Mother was on her way to the 'mourners bench'.

The taxi pulled up in front of the church. 'Is that it?' my mother asked incredulously.

'Lady, that's it.' The taxi driver switched his cigar from one corner of his mouth to the other.

We all stared. I giggled. The front windows of the small store building had been decorated to look like stained glass windows. 'It looks like a fortune-telling place,' I said. 'Look at the lighthouse up on the corner of the building!' A small toy-like lighthouse valiantly flashed light to a dark world.

'I don't know,' my mother wavered.

'Good, let's go home.' Dad seemed to know what to do.

'Wait, Mrs Murphy,' said Marie, the waitress who came along. 'You really should go in. I've seen churches like this before. We have them down south in Georgia. They're holy roller churches. They're really a ball! You don't want to miss it!'

My mother stiffened. 'No siree, we don't laugh at anybody's religion. I was always taught that. They might be right and we might be wrong. If we go in there, none of us will laugh, hear me?' She glanced my way, for I was already showing interest in the prospects of a giggling good time.

The taxi driver spoke up. 'Lady, are you going in or ain't cha?' The ticking meter seemed to sound louder.

'All right, we're going in, but no laughing.'

We all piled out towards the doors of the new church. They swung open as if they operated on a seeing eye. No doubt several eyes had been peeking through the cracks in the decorated glass door.

'Good evening, we're glad to see you.' Our hands were shaken as though we were long lost cousins. Down the only aisle we were ushered with pleasure and pride. Songbooks were thrust into our hands and suddenly the little room was full of joyous noise as people clapped and sang 'Whosoever will, may come'.

'This is great,' I thought. I settled down to enjoy myself, looking forward to the swinging on the chandeliers and the dancing down the aisles that Marie had predicted.

Suddenly I sensed Mother's disapproval. It sizzled down the whole row of us who were crowded into the brown-painted pew.

'What's wrong?' Dad asked. Mother was staring straight ahead at five Negro singers who were in the front row.

'I never sat in church with niggers before,' she said with stiff lips. 'I don't intend to sit with them now!' For all her generosity, Mother was a southerner full of deep racial prejudice. She carried it with her when they moved from the south to the north and it still throbbed in her heart. My Dad, who was usually the first to agree with my mother, displayed a strong, stubborn resistance that I had never seen before. Putting his feet across the end of the row between the pews, he muttered firmly out of the side of his mouth, 'You drug us in here and you're not draggin' us out!' Mother looked at him quickly, saw the set of his chin and settled down. She really wanted to stay.

'We are pleased to have with us this evening the Flying Cloud Quartet from Detroit, Michigan,' a man announced from the platform. The Blacks sang as only Blacks can. Their rich voices harmonized to tell the story of their Savior. Mother began to melt under the charm of their smiles and their obvious sincerity.

Then the blonde evangelist stood, dressed in a long white gown, and began her sermon. 'My subject tonight is "Who's Who in Hell".'

'Wow!' I thought. 'That's a pretty direct approach and right on the bullseye for my mother with all her worries about hell, and all that.'

It seemed as though the whole thing had been especially planned for Mother. I even spied a long bench across the front of the platform that must have been a 'mourners' bench'. I thought, 'Here's a church like the one my mother's been looking for, after all.'

The evangelist's voice was soft. The call was being given for those needing prayer to raise their hands. 'Thank you. God bless you,' she said as hands were raised all over the congregation.

'Mother will surely put her hand up,' I thought. 'This is it!'

'Anyone else?' The evangelist waited. Out of the corner of my eye I saw Mother's hand go up. As if we had been waiting for the signal, up went our hands—mine, Dad's, and all the rest who had come with us.

'Now, will you stand right where you are. In a moment we are going to meet at this altar,' (they didn't call it a 'mourner's bench'!) 'and we are going to accept the Lord, ask for forgiveness of our sins and allow him to change our lives.' Others moved forward but Mother kept her seat. We all sat waiting to see what would happen next. To our shock the evangelist left the platform and came towards us! Someone led a hymn as she came directly to my mother. 'I saw your raised hand,' she said smiling. Her voice was gentle. 'I'm sure you want to accept the Lord, don't you?' Holding back the tears, Mother nodded her head. 'Won't you come forward, then? I should like to pray for you.' Mother couldn't speak, but definitely shook her head 'no'.

'What's wrong with her?' I was annoyed. 'If she had said "yes", I'd have gone right up with her.' The evangelist looked quickly at the rest of us. Every head shook negative!

'I understand,' the evangelist said kindly. 'I'm sure you want to think over such an important step. Is this the first time you've been in a service like this?'

'Yes,' Mother managed to say.

The evangelist squeezed my mother's hand. I'm sure you won't mind if I promise to pray for you and invite you to return, will you?' Mother couldn't say a word, but her tearful smile said 'yes' for all of us.

Later at home, as we drank coffee and rehearsed all that happened that night, Mother said, 'there's one thing sure. I know that woman cares about my soul.'

Over the next few days my mind wouldn't let go of the evangelist's words, 'On Wednesday night there will be prayer for the sick. Jesus Christ is the same yesterday, and today, and forever.' By that Wednesday evening we had decided to return. We didn't tell Dr. Brady what we planned to do, but I was carefully wrapped up, lifted into the taxi and, along with another taxi full of friends from the restaurant, we went across the city of Toledo, Ohio, back to that strange little church with its blinking lighthouse. It looked beautiful!

A concerned usher looked into my swollen face. I could scarcely see out of my puffed-up eyes. 'Could the evangelist see my daughter now and help her?' my mother asked. He hurried away and returned with the message that the evangelist thought it best that we hear the sermon first. We were told that faith came by hearing the Word of God. I couldn't concentrate on anything that was said. The moment came when all those who were sick were invited to come forward for prayer. The place was packed. Many other sick people had come, crowding the tiny church.

'I'll never make it,' I thought. Then I stood. It seemed as though hands were under my elbows lifting me. I was moving towards the front where the evangelist waited. I tried to see where my dad was. He was still sitting in the pew.

'You expect me to heal you?' the evangelist asked when I reached her.

'Yes,' I replied, feeling that this was the time for the right answers.

'I'm sorry, but I can't heal you.'

'What a fake!' I thought. Anger exploded in my head. 'I've read about this sort of thing. Here I am because she invited the sick to come, but when there's someone really ill like me, it's all off!'

Her voice continued. 'You see, I'm like a waitress. Do you know what a waitress is?'

A waitress! I'd served tables for my mother in her restaurant since I'd been tall enough to reach the counter. Did this woman know this? There was no way for her to know. We lived on the other side of the city and we had not filled out a visitor's card. She didn't even know our names!

She continued. 'A customer comes into a restaurant and selects a meal from the menu. Then the waitress takes the order to the chef and he prepares it. When it's ready, the waitress serves it to the hungry customer. Do you understand this?' she asked.

'Yes.' I understood everything that far. Why was she doing this?

'Well, I'm a servant of the Lord. Your need, or order, is for the healing of your kidneys. I'm going to take your need to the Lord in prayer. He will send his healing power. All I'll do is serve to you what the Lord Jesus has given. Do you see? I can't heal you but he can and he will. Can you believe this?'

'Yes, I can believe that.' She had directed my attention from herself to the Great Physician. She prayed a simple prayer, laying hands on my head as she prayed. I'd expected a much longer prayer. I stood waiting. Suddenly I felt something like a slight shock go through me. The pain stopped. I knew I was healed. 'Praise the Lord!' she said.

By the time I returned home that night, my temperature was normal. The next day I dressed and went to see my doctor, instead of his coming to see me. All the swelling had gone. The infection had disappeared. 'What are you doing out of bed?' he demanded.

'I'm healed!' I answered. While he sat staring in disbelief, I told him what had happened.

'You'll go into the hospital and we'll find out if you're healed or not,' he said impatiently. 'You know how kidney trouble is—one day up and the next day down.' After two days of extensive tests in the hospital every x-ray and examination showed that I was not only healed of the infection, but that the kidney that had been smaller and non-functioning was now the same size as the other one and both were functioning normally!

As they said at the hospital, it looked like I had a miracle!

CHAPTER TWO

WE DECEIVE OURSELVES

The full reality of what had happened hit me hard when I got home from the hospital. The mental reaction set in. God had given me a miracle! The first time anyone had asked God to give me a miracle, there it was! It wasn't like I had sought him all that much. It was really Mother's quest that I had found myself caught up in. I hadn't been exactly troubled about my soul. Even the prospect of death had not sent me to my knees. In fact, nothing had really happened until I heard the evangelist preach.

A strong sense of gratitude began to fill my heart. I began to feel obligated to God for the first time in years. During my childhood I had sought to find ways to please God. I had always wanted to do something for him, to show him my appreciation. Now, I desired to do something more than ever. But what could I do for God? I began to reason with myself. If he hadn't healed me, I would probably have died. So, why not offer him the rest of my life in order to serve him somehow? Then I wondered, how could I serve him?

Be a nun, a missionary? That's it! I'll go back to that little church and offer to be a missionary. It was only right to do so, I decided. Why, God should be delighted to have such a grateful person with all my potential coming back to offer my services! I was exhilarated, I wanted to shout, 'Heaven here I come!'

Yet I knew shouting at God was hardly the proper approach. How does one give one's life to God? I pondered. Well, I continued to reason, since I am going to make this offer to God, I suppose a prayer is the proper way. So I wrote out a neat Methodist, Baptist, Lutheran, Presbyterian prayer, using some vocabulary I had learned from each of them. I ended up with one of the most smug statements of self-righteousness ever composed by a teenager.

At last I was going to please God! My parents and I returned, with our friends, to the church the next night. There were services every night. When the sermon ended and the invitation was given, I was ready to go forward with my written prayer, which I had memorized fairly well. Kneeling at the plain wooden bench, I began to say my prayer. An uneasiness crept over me. I felt I was being irreverent. I couldn't say the words—they seemed to stick in my throat. I looked around bewildered, wondering what I had done wrong. For some inexplicable reason it seemed I had insulted God. A short, round-faced woman with long, brown hair braided neatly around her head, knelt beside me. Leaning towards me, she smiled and asked, 'Can I help you?'

'I don't seem able to pray,' I faltered.

'Let me show you a scripture,' she offered. Opening her Bible she laid it before me and pointed to the words 'If we say we have no sin, we deceive ourselves, and the truth is not in us.'

'You see, first we must confess that we are sinners,' she explained. 'We must be honest with the Lord, not fooling ourselves.' She moved on to the next verse 'If we confess our sins…'

'Oh I've done that,' I broke in. 'Ever since I knew how, I've confessed to God at the end of the day the sins I knew I had committed, and even asked him to forgive the ones I couldn't remember.'

She smiled. 'You know, every time you confessed I'm sure he forgave you, but, you see, there is more to salvation than just being forgiven of your sins. There are many people who go to church and confess their sins every week or, like you, they confess them each day, but they commit those same sins again—the same ones, over and over.'

I knew what she meant. Sometimes it was monotonous how I had to ask God to forgive me for the same thing again and again. It was embarrassing, too.

'Let me explain,' my helper continued, as we settled into a comfortable position beside the altar. 'Say I have a little girl, and I get her all cleaned up for church. While I'm dressing myself, she may go out and play. Then, suddenly she comes in crying, covered with dirt. You see, she's fallen in a mud puddle. Now all she says is, "I'm sorry", but don't you think I would forgive her?'

'Of course,' I replied.

'That's right, but that's not all I would do. I would also change her clothes and wash her, for her sake and for mine. That is what God has promised here. He says that the Lord Jesus is faithful and just to forgive you and to cleanse you from all unrighteousness. He not only wants to forgive you but to cleanse you—to take away your sins, so you don't have to keep asking him again and again to forgive the same old things. He'll take the old desires and habits away completely.'

She suggested that I not only ask for forgiveness but also to be cleansed from my sin. Well, this wasn't what I had intended to do when I came! I had come to make God an offer—one good turn deserved another, sort of thing. Now he had switched it around and I had to admit that I had nothing to offer but my sinful self. Yet it seemed right and I had to face the truth.

As I prayed, tears of repentance flowed and relief flooded into my heart, I knew that I was forgiven and cleansed. I was different inside and I wanted to shout out to all the world, 'I've had another miracle!'

Dad was next. He saw the change in me and began to wonder if God couldn't give him a new set of lungs, as well as a new heart. Dad was completely healed and was soon telling everyone about his new-found Saviour. A war-time buddy of his met him on the street after his conversion and stared at him in amazement. 'John Murphy, what has happened to you?'

'I'm a new man,' Dad replied, ready to go on and tell the story to his old friend.

Smitty stopped him. 'But the American Legion told the undertaker to get your casket ready. It didn't look like it would be too long before you needed it.'

Dad laughed. 'Smitty, I'm looking for the uppertaker, not the undertaker!'

Dad and I and many of our friends were changed by the power of God. Mother had brought us all to the mourners' bench, and now we were full of joy. That is everyone but Mother!

Mother had a problem. Everybody who knew her was aware of it. She was like a bomb with a long fuse. Her Irish temper stayed under control during long periods of aggravation, but when she did explode her language left the air blue. Though generally gentle and soft-spoken, she could swear like a sailor.

Night after night during the summer of our salvation, Grace Murphy would gather more and more of her friends to go hear the gospel preached. Most of her employees were converted. Marie, the waitress who first talked us into getting out of the taxi and entering the little store-fronted church, was dramatically converted. For years she had suffered at night with tortuous dreams of hell. After her confession and conversion she could lay he head down in peace. Her husband, a long lanky Georgian nicknamed Limbertwig, was a shiftless drunkard who could easily sit with his heels resting on the edge of the heating stove reading Zane Grey westerns while the fire went out. Then he'd order Marie to bring in more coal. Marie's wages were usually going to bail him out of jail. One night Limbertwig came to church with Marie. He was so powerfully gripped with conviction that he grasped the pew in front of him with white-knuckled desperation. The pew shook and rattled under his trembling. Finally, he let go and fairly ran to pray at the precious place we had all learned to love, the altar.

'Mother,' I asked, 'why don't you go, too?'

Tears were on her face as she watched Limbertwig praying at the altar. 'I can't, she said, shaking her head.

Later at home, as we ate our after-church snack in the kitchen, I pressed the point. 'Why not Mother?'

'Jean,' she paused to pour buttermilk into a tall glass. 'You know what a temper I have.' She began to butter a square of yellow cornbread.

'No more than the rest of us,' I reminded her. We Murphys were a pretty hot-headed lot. 'But Jesus has changed us. Look how he's helped Dad. Why he is not nearly so nervous and irritable. He doesn't even need to smoke any more.'

'Yes, I know, but there's my swearing. I picked up those words when I was young. Being an orphan, I got knocked around a lot by the kind of people I had to live with. It's so deep in me. I don't think I could ever stop myself from swearing when I get mad. When the orders get all messed up at the restaurant I lose my temper. What will the others say if they hear me swearing? If I go up to that altar they'll expect me to be different. I don't want to be a hypocrite.' Pushing back her chair abruptly, she gathered up the dishes and started towards the sink. 'One thing I don't want to be, that's a hypocrite. If I'm going to be a Christian, I want to be a real one.'

'Mother, if God can give me new kidneys, and Dad a new set of lungs, and sober up Limbertwig, don't you think he can give you a new tongue?'

She stared at me a moment, turned and plunged her hands into the dishwater. I reached for the dishtowel and said no more.

The next night the sermon text was timely: 'For by grace you have been saved through faith; and this is not your own doing; it is the gift of God, not of works, lest any man should boast. For we are his workmanship, created in Christ Jesus for good works, which God prepared beforehand, that we should walk in them.'

'Now your righteousness,' the evangelist summed up, 'the Bible says, is as filthy rags. Salvation is not a result of your own efforts. Don't try to fix yourself up. Don't wait until you think you are able to live it. You'll never make it. Come as you are and let Christ change you into a new creature. Then you'll be able to walk as he wants you to walk and talk as he wants you to talk. His righteousness will change your life. Take the step of faith.'

Suddenly, Mother started moving. Since she weighed about two hundred pounds, she wasn't able to slip unnoticed past the others in the pew. Six people had to move into the aisle to make room for her. That made no difference. She was past the point of excuses or embarrassment. She was soon kneeling at her long-sought-after mourners' bench, her pride at last bowed.

A few days later, a new waitress came out of the restaurant kitchen looking perplexed. 'Hey,' she drew aside another waitress. 'That Mrs. Murphy is a funny woman.'

'What do you mean?'

She glanced back where Mother was standing near the steam table, red-faced but smiling. 'Well,' the new girl went on, 'I've just messed up a big order. Everything got mixed up. I was afraid to tell her, but I had to. She stood there staring at all those wrong orders. I thought I was going to get fired. Then she just looked up and said, "Praise the Lord!" Figure that out, will you?'

CHAPTER THREE

THE SPIRIT...
IS UPON ME

It was an unusually hot spring day when we went to Walbridge Park on Memorial Day, May 30th. It was a perfect day to be baptised in the Maumee River! Yes, I was going to be baptised again! I'd decided that, since I was not born again when I was baptised before, I really ought to go through the ceremony again. Besides, my Mother and Dad were going to be baptised and we wanted to go together as a family into the experience. We wanted the world to know that we had been to the cross and died there to the old life. When we went into that 'watery grave' we were determined to leave behind the old life and to rise with newness of life with the victory of the risen Lord. It was a happy day.

Hundreds stood on the shores, forgetting their picnic lunches. Bathers swam in closer, treading water, to watch the strange sight of scores of people dressed in white walking into the water. Families and young people in canoes

31

and boats drew in until it seemed as though we were re-enacting a scene at the Jordan when Jesus had stood in the waters and said to John, 'Thus it is fitting for us.'

'Upon the confession of your faith, I now baptise you in the name of the Father and of the Son and of the Holy Spirit.' Splash! The waters sounded as though they were laughing with joy as we went down, submissive to the hands of the evangelist and a helpful pastor who immersed us. 'Hallelujah!' the Christians shouted on shore. 'Hallelujah!' the preachers said smiling.

I blinked away the water that glistened like diamonds before my eyes, raised both hands with my mother and father and we shouted, 'Hallelujah!'

We waded back to shore. I could hear the jeers and laughter of those who couldn't understand the sign that was being given them. In the crowd there was one who wasn't laughing. Several days after the baptismal service our pastor received a letter from a stranger, saying that she had come to the river that day with the intention of committing suicide. The sight of people who had found enough meaning in their lives to so openly manifest it, had changed her plans and her destiny. She sought a place alone and prayed for the first time in many years.

We changed and rolled up our wet clothes and towels. I had never felt so clean, inside and out. The evangelist, LaDonna Dalrymple, came over to our car. 'The pastor who helped me baptise is having a special meeting in his church tonight,' she said. 'Why don't you go? I can't go myself, but a number of those who where baptised will be there.' Eager to please her and always wanting to hear more about Jesus, we consented.

That evening we were seated in the big tabernacle. Except for the barnlike size, it was not much different to the store building church we had learned to love so much. There was an informal air. Everyone seemed to know one another. The singing was bright. Then, things began to change. The shouting increased in volume. The music grew louder, and people began to get up from their seats and dance in the aisles. I turned to my parents and they were looking at me. We all had one question, 'Why did Mrs. Dalrymple suggest we come here?' There were testimonies that lasted longer than the sermons we usually heard. These were interspersed with the most active singing I had ever seen. Emotionalism was bursting out on all sides. Some laughed, some wept, some stood up with their hands in the air, and others danced. One man ran around the place waving his arms and sounding for all the world like a diesel locomotive!

'Here,' I thought, 'is the holy roller church that the waitress told us about!' We had never seen this before. Just about the time my father nervously suggested we should go home, the pastor announced that he felt 'led of the Lord' not to preach that night. Since it was eleven o'clock I inwardly agreed that it was a good idea. I think it was the only time in the service that I had thanked God!

We rose to leave, hoping to get out before the last song and dance. The sonorous voice of the pastor sounded out. 'All those who want more of the Lord, come up front now before you go home. It's been a great day and you've got a lot to thank the Lord for.' He seemed to be looking right at us. It had been a great day. We obeyed and went forward. 'We'll just pray a few minutes and leave,' Mother whispered. More people crowded in and I nodded my head 'yes', looking towards the door. Mother and Dad went to the far side of the wide tabernacle. I knelt at the opposite end of the altar space on the bare brown floor, resting my elbows on the opera seat in the first row. The altar was full of praying people. The piano played on, drums were beating and tambourines jangled. Voices in song and loud prayer rose like the sound of a roaring cataract.

Then I heard it. How I heard it I'll never know. It was so soft, like a murmuring brook, almost imperceptible. I listened, afraid I would lose it. Someone's voice praying in a foreign language. I turned with my fingers spread out over my eyes to allow me to watch and pray! There, almost beside me, knelt a woman in a cheap cotton print housedress. Both her hands were extended, palms up, as if she were reaching for a gift. Her eyes were closed and her face was raised towards the ceiling, or towards heaven. She was so enraptured in her worship of the Lord she was unaware of all the commotion around her. I glanced to see if a bright light was shining anywhere upon her face, which was aglow with a golden glory. It came from inside, not outside. I couldn't understand a word she said, but I knew she was worshipping and praising God, loving him as I longed to do. I presumed that she was speaking Polish since we were in a neighbourhood of Polish people.

Within my heart I asked, 'Heavenly Father, I don't know what that lady has inside her, but I'm sure it's what causes her face to shine and helps her to pray like that. I'd like to pray like that, to be so enthralled with you that I wouldn't notice anything around, to love you and praise you that way. I've so much to praise you for, and it's so hard for me to express my joy and love to you. If what she has is real—and I think it is—and if it's for me, then please Lord, give it to me.'

I felt the presence of Jesus around me closer and closer, within me fuller and fuller. My heart was melted by His love. Tears flowed down my cheeks. I wanted to put my hands out as the little lady beside me did. I lifted them and they seemed to be taken by the hands of Jesus. They trembled and my lips trembled as I began to praise him. Words flowed like a river from my heart. Suddenly I realised I was speaking in a language I had never learned. I knew then that the little lady with the shining face was not speaking Polish. It was a language of love flowing from the heart. Somewhere deep within me a river of joy had begun to flow and I hoped it would never stop.

Over an hour later, after the music had all stopped and quietness had settled all around me, I reluctantly opened my eyes. Mother and Dad were looking at me in bewilderment. Concern was written all over their faces. No one said anything. I looked at the pastor who was standing with the door keys in his hand. He stepped over to help me to my feet and shaking my hand he beamed, 'Well, sister, you got it. Believe me, you got it!' I was still too overpowered with the presence of the lord to ask any questions. Dad slipped his arm around me, patting my shoulder. 'It's all right, honey,' he said, 'you'll be all right in the morning.'

The pastor was turning out the lights. We walked slowly toward the door as Mother and Dad supported me. My knees were wobbly—I was drunk! That night as I lay in bed still praising the Lord in the strange language, I heard my parents say outside my door, 'If she isn't over this by morning, we'll call the doctor.'

Mother and Dad watched me nervously as I poured the cornflakes into the bowl next morning. I bowed my head and prayed in English! I could hear them both sigh with relief. After I had finished eating, Mother said, 'Young lady, we're going to take you out to see Mrs. Dalrymple. She is more likely to be able to tell what happened to you last night than the Presbyterian pastor.' Although I still went to the Presbyterian church on Sunday morning, I was quite sure my mother was right. Weeks before when I had told the Presbyterian pastor about my healing and conversion, he had remarked, 'Oh, you'll get over it.' 'Over it!' I had exclaimed. ' I don't want to get over it. I was dying before this happened to me!'

We met Mrs. Dalrymple at the door of the little church with the lighthouse. She seemed surprised to see us, but pleased. I wasn't so sure I was pleased to see her, though. On the way to the church I had begun to feel worried. What had happened to me last night? How could I describe it? I was reluctant to tell Mrs. Dalrymple about it. What if she said it was wrong? Could it have been emotionalism? Was it even possible that something evil had happened?

Mother gave me a gentle shove. 'Go ahead, tell Mrs. Dalrymple exactly what happened to you last night.'

'Well, we went to the tabernacle like you asked us to do. Afterwards we went up to pray at the front. I began to praise the Lord and before I knew what was happening...' I hesitated. The evangelist smiled at me and said, 'Yes, go on.'

'Well, I started to pray in a language I'd never learned. I had never spoken those words before. They just seemed to roll off my tongue.'

'Jean, the Lord baptised you with the Holy Spirit!' the evangelist exclaimed.

'Did he?' I asked. She looked at my mother and father and then it dawned on her.

'Don't you know what the baptism of the Holy Spirit is?'

'No,' we all three said at once. It wasn't long before she had her Bible out and began to tell us about the person of the Godhead called the Holy Spirit. She had scriptures marked all the way through from Genesis to Revelation.

She began to explain. 'To understand what the baptism of the Holy Spirit is you need to know who the Holy Spirit is. He is a person, co-equal, co-eternal with the Father and the Son. Why, he is co-author of this very Book, the Word of God,' she said. 'Look, it says here in 2 Peter 1:21 "No prophecy ever came by the impulse of man, but men moved by the Holy Spirit spoke from God..."' Then turning to Genesis, she continued, 'He was there with the Father and the Son when they said, "Let us make man in our own image." He seemed to be there for a special purpose, to help bring the earth out of chaos into divine light and order.' I read the underlined words in her Bible, 'And the Spirit of God was moving over the face of the waters.'

'He is a creative spirit,' the evangelist went on. 'He quickens and gives life. Right from the beginning he was on a mission from the Father to man. He seemed intent upon drawing men to God. In the Old Testament he changed men. Those who surrendered to him became prophets, priests and kings.' We looked quickly in the Old Testament at Moses, Aaron, Elisha, David, Gideon and Samson.

Flicking the pages of her well-worn Bible she continued, 'We see the Holy Spirit as creator at the beginning of the New Testament too. He was there in creative power when the angel said to Mary, "The Holy Spirit will come upon you" (Luke 1:35). Jesus was conceived by the Holy Spirit.'

'At his baptism in the river Jordan, the Godhead was manifested in the beauty of perfect unity. The Father spoke, as described in Matthew 3:17, "This is my beloved Son, in whom I am well pleased", and the Holy Spirit descended upon the Son like a dove. Just as the anointing oil had flowed upon the prophets and priests of the Old Testament, when they were empowered to serve God, so "God anointed Jesus of Nazareth with the Holy Spirit and with power." We read

in Acts 10:38, the result of that anointing. Read it, Jean.'
Looking closer I read, '...how God anointed Jesus of
Nazareth with the Holy Ghost and with power, who went
about doing good and healing all that were oppressed of
the devil.'

'You see, when Jesus began preaching, he was introduced
by John in Matthew 3:11 as the one who "will baptise you
with the Holy Spirit and with fire".' As Jesus came closer
and closer to the cross, he made stronger and clearer prom-
ises about the Holy Spirit coming to his followers. For in-
stance, we read here in Luke 11:13, "If you then, who are
evil, know how to give good gifts to your children, how
much more will the heavenly Father give the Holy Spirit to
those who ask him!", and John 14:16,17, "And I will pray
the Father, and he will give you another Counsellor, to be
with you forever, even the Spirit of truth, whom the world
cannot receive, because it neither sees him nor knows him;
you know him, for he dwells with you, and will be in you."

'After his death on the cross and his resurrection, he
gave this instruction and promise to his followers, "Behold,
I send the promise of my Father upon you; but stay in the
city, until you are clothed with power from high," (Luke
24:49) and "But you shall receive power when the Holy
Spirit has come upon you; and you shall be my witnesses
in Jerusalem and in all Judea and Samaria and to the end of
the earth" (Acts 1:8). So. After Jesus had ascended, his followers waited in Jerusalem in the upper room. It was there
that they received the promise, as it shows us in Acts 2:4,
"And they were all filled with the Holy Spirit and began to
speak in tongues, as the Spirit gave them utterance."'

'Why,' I exclaimed, 'that is what happened to me last
night.'

'Exactly,' LaDonna Dalrymple said. 'You received power as Jesus promised in Acts 1:8. So have I and most of the members of this church. This experience is for every believer. For the promise is to everyone. Read it here in Acts 2:39.' Mother and Dad and I read the promise. 'That is why you were healed, Jean, because through the gift of the Holy Spirit we ministered to you in Jesus' name. The one who healed you is also the Baptiser in the Holy Ghost.'

'Then I have received power to serve the Lord; to be a witness,' I said, deeply moved. 'But there is something that bothers me. Last night when we went to that church the people behaved so differently to the way they do here.' We described their actions. 'It was so emotional, yet it was the place where I received this experience. Was what they were doing pleasing to the Lord?'

'Jean, you were looking at those people through the eyes of a new Christian who's never seen a service like that before. I only have your impressions to go by. You may interpret them quite differently some other time. I wasn't there, so I can't say. However, let me explain something to you. The power of the Holy Spirit is like the steam in a locomotive.' I thought of the man, the night before, who had run around in the tabernacle waving his arms and sounding like a diesel! 'You see, that power can be used to pull the train down the track. The train can carry goods and passengers to many places. It really depends upon the engineer as to what he does with that power. He could just sit at the station and blow the whistle until there's no power left.

'Jesus said, "As the Father sent me, so send I you." The purpose of Pentecost is to take the powerful, loving ministry of Jesus into all the world.

'God has given us gifts and he tells us how to use them.' She showed us Paul's teaching in 1 Corinthians chapters

12 and 14. 'Be sure you honour the Holy Spirit,' she emphasised. 'Paul warns us never to quench him (1 Thessalonians 5: 19) and never to grieve him (Ephesians 4:30). If you honour him, then he will honour you with his ministry.'

Mrs. Dalrymple paused, looking at me intently. 'There are times to "blow the whistle", Jean. We need to praise the Lord with the power of the Holy Spirit. Chiefly, it is for us to pray in the Spirit and to go in the power of the Spirit, taking blessings to people wherever he leads us. He will "teach us all things" (John 14:26) and he will "guide us into all truth" (John 16:13).' She took my hands in hers. 'I feel that he is going to take you to many parts of the world and you will have gifts to give to many.' She laid her hands on my head and prayed. Once again I felt full of the Holy Spirit.

I could hardly wait to tell my pastor at the Presbyterian Church about the power of the Holy Spirit coming upon me. His cool reaction to my healing and conversion had been so baffling to me. But here was something that had happened to me just as it had happened in Acts. Surely he couldn't deny such a biblical experience.

'Why, Jean,' he exclaimed after I had finished, 'that's not for today! That,' he waved his hand as if to shoo away the whole thing, 'was for the apostles.'

I was rocked. 'What am I going to do? I've already got it.'

We stared at each other. He finally said, slowly, as if he was terribly tired, 'Jean, I suggest that you go back to that place where you claim you were healed. I think they could help you more than I on these matters.'

Thanking him for his good advice, I left.

CHAPTER FOUR

RAISE THE DEAD

We were told by Christian friends that we should have a family altar in our home. The Pentecostal pastor explained that it was the place where we came together as a family to pray. It could be anywhere in the house. The main thing was that we met regularly to read the Bible and to pray together. So the kitchen table became the altar and after breakfast was the time. There we talked freely with one another and with God about everything.

One Sunday morning we pushed back the empty coffee cups and waited before the Lord. During the prayer time he showed something startling to my mother. She knew something unusual was going to happen that day which would drastically affect all three of us, but she didn't tell us. It was good that she didn't tell us. We could not have accepted it as she did.

She tried to tell our pastor after the morning service. At the church door she asked if she could talk to him about something important. I was standing nearby as she stepped aside with him. 'I want you to know what I'd like done

41

about Jean…' Glancing towards me she stopped and asked me to go wait in the car. 'Tell your dad that I'll be there in just a minute.' She knew how impatient Dad would be to get home. He had a ravenous appetite since his lungs had been healed and he no longer smoked. He was anxious for his Sunday dinner; usually southern fried chicken, fluffy sour milk biscuits and country milk chicken gravy, green beans cooked with bacon and for dessert, hot apple pie.

'What's she talking so long about?' he asked after waiting five minutes.

'I don't know. She won't be long,' I said, wondering myself what it was all about. What was she asking the pastor to do about me?

Dad leaned on the horn. 'She'd take all day if I didn't blow the horn', he said. Mother hurried out to the car. Pastor Allan stood in the entrance of the church looking perplexed.

She seemed anxious to get dinner over and excused herself to get aside to pray. The afternoon went by uneventfully. Soon we were off again to the church for the Sunday evening service. As soon as it was over Mother tried to have a few more minutes with the pastor, but he was busy and Dad was hungry again. So we went home.

While Dad raided the refrigerator for leftovers, Mother got ready for bed. Suddenly I felt a strong urge to go into her bedroom. Maybe she would like to talk about whatever it was that she had tried to tell Pastor Allan.

'Hi!' I poked my head around the door. 'Mind if I come in?' Mother was in her nightgown, kneeling by her bed.

'Honey, come in and kneel and pray with me.' She patted the chenille bedspread. I picked up a soft cushion and placed it on the linoleum floor close to her. We prayed together, united in our faith and concern for those we both loved. Then she stopped praying aloud. I waited. The room was very quiet. I decided she wanted to be alone, perhaps to pray about whatever had been on her mind all day. I tiptoed to the bedroom door. Glancing back before I shut the door, I was startled to see that she had slumped into a very unnatural position. She looked odd—slightly grotesque. I rushed back. 'Mother!' I shook her. She fell limply against me. As I stepped back alarmed, she slipped down on the floor unconscious, or was she dead! She looked so strange; the vacant non-expression on her face.

'Dad, Dad,' I shouted down the long narrow hall towards the kitchen. 'Dad, come quick. Mother...she's unconscious. I think she's...She looks awful!'

Dad slammed the refrigerator door and came running. He helped me lift her on to the bed. We were so awkward. She was a big-boned woman, weighing over two hundred pounds. Her body was helplessly limp.

'Better go get Marie next door,' Dad said with a tight voice. He was afraid. Before I reached the door he had started dialing the phone numbers of the doctor and the pastor.

'Marie's a registered nurse and she'll know just what do do,' I thought as she and I rushed into the bedroom. I expected the nightmare to be over in a minute. Marie would examine Mother carefully and tell us not to worry...everything would be all right. She looked up and spoke softly to Dad, 'Grace is gone, John.' I gasped. Marie put her arms around me. 'Jesus has taken your mother home to be with him, Jean.' I pulled away and dropped to my knees, sobbing. She started to pull the sheet over mother's face. Dad fell across the bed, snatching it back. He softly slapped Mother's face. 'Grace, Grace you can't go. Grace, wake up, wake up.' 'Jesus,' I cried out, 'don't take my mother from me. Bring her back. Bring my mother back to me.' I was in a corner with my face to the floor.

Marie answered the insistent ringing doorbell. Our pastor, the Rev. Allan, rushed in. 'She's dead,' Marie whispered.

'Mr. Murphy, come, get a hold of yourself—This is a great shock, but when a Christian dies it is a triumph, not a tragedy.' Pastor Allan led my dad to a chair. Dad stared in disbelief at my mother. He said nothing.

Then Pastor Allan continued, speaking to all of us, 'This is one of the most unusual things I have ever seen happen in all my years of pastoring. Mrs. Murphy tried to tell me this morning that she knew she was going to go to be with the Lord today. She wanted me to know and she was concerned about what would happen to both of you. Frankly, I could hardly believe what she was saying. It was so strange discussing funeral arrangements just like she knew for sure it was to happen today. She said the Lord had told her this morning during your family altar. Why, it is a marvelous thing. This is remarkable. I never saw a Christian die this way.'

'No, no, I can't let her go,' I wept. 'We need her so.' Anxiety flooded my mind. What would happen now? Would Dad go on serving the Lord? He depended so much upon Mother. How would I cope? I was fifteen years old. What would happen after I graduated from high school? These were unreasonable fears and my selfish heart would not let me listen to the reasonings of my pastor nor Marie. I prayed all the harder, 'Oh please, Jesus, bring my mother back to me.'

Pastor Allan knelt beside me. 'Jean, your faith is very strong. Don't use it to rob your mother of heaven now. She

accepted God's will fully, can't you? She has God's perfect
will. Don't force yourselves into something less than that.' I
prayed all the more. I would not let her go. 'Bring my mother
back to me,' I cried out. My words echoed in the strange
silence that followed. Minutes ticked by. No one seemed
able to speak. We seemed to be waiting for something. I sat
with my head buried in my hands. I didn't want to look up
and see her there...looking so separated from us.

Dad's voice broke the silence. 'Look, look at her eyes.'
He raised up out of the chair. We all looked. Her eyelids
were fluttering, shattering the glassy stare. Then they closed.
Had we seen her eyelids flutter or were we imagining it?
'Her lips are moving,' Marie whispered. No sound, only a
movement. Stunned, we watched. She slowly turned her
head. She opened her eyes and looked at me. I felt she was
looking at me form the other side of the grave. Softly, sadly,
she spoke. 'Why did you bring me back?' Her eyes closed
again. I looked at Pastor Allan. I knew his word had been
true. Dad still stared at Mother's face. Marie hurried over to
take her pulse. The doorbell rang.

Dr. Brady rushed us out of the room, especially when
he saw me kneeling by the bed, my face swollen from weeping. 'Take her out of here,' he told Dad. Marie stayed to
help him examine Mother. 'Mr. Murphy, come in,' Dr. Brady
called out. Mother had suffered a major heart attack. It
seemed to be ruptured and there were signs of a massive
hemorrhage. 'I must warn you,' I overheard him say, 'she
may not last the night. I really don't understand how she
has survived this long. I'll phone back every hour, and you
phone sooner if you need me.'

Each time he phoned, Dad would report that Mother
was resting and her breathing was normal. Finally, about
five a.m., the doctor phoned again. 'How is she?' Dad said,

'She is getting more rest than any of us. I'll call you if I need you.'

For several days, Mother was reluctant to talk or eat. Mostly, she slept. When she was awake we could hardly interest her in anything. Gradually, she regained her strength and responded to what was going on around her.

When she was able to walk, we led her into the living room to sit by the window. I drew up a footstool so I could sit close to her knee. 'Mother, what happened that night? Do you want to talk about it?'

'Yes, honey, I'm ready now. You see, it started that Sunday morning. While I was praying I seemed to know without a doubt that I was going to be with the Lord that day.'

I interrupted, 'Didn't you feel sad? I mean, how could you think of leaving Dad and me? Didn't that worry you?'

'No, I didn't feel sad nor glad. It seemed so certain and final. I had no choice, so I accepted it. I was concerned about you. I seemed to know you'd be all right. I knew it was God's will. But I did try to talk to Pastor Allan about you. Remember when I stopped to talk at the church door after service?' I nodded. 'All day I expected it. Then, when you came in to pray with me, I felt the Lord was very near and He had sent you to be with me. As we prayed I saw Jesus. He walked into the room and came towards me saying, "Grace, I've come to take you home."'

'I didn't see him,' I broke in.

'I know,' Mother said.

Mother recalled how happy she had felt when she heard him speak her name. She was completely resigned to his will, she said. Then, he touched her head and she felt her spirit leave her body. 'I was like a child again. I felt like a nine-year-old.' She paused. 'You know, that was the age I was when I first sought the Lord in that old-fashioned Methodist camp meeting.'

She explained how weightless, unburdened and free she seemed after that transition. There were no tensions, anxieties, no pain, no weariness.

'I was a child standing by my Saviour. He held my hand. I had a momentary glance at my old body slumped by the bed and I saw you kneeling there. In the next instant, the world was gone. Everything disappeared. We were standing in a different realm. It was strange and we were surrounded by darkness. The darkness extended as far as I could see, except where Jesus and I stood.

'How desolate it would have been if Jesus had not been there. At our feet was light. It was a thread of light extending upward as far as I could see. Jesus and I began to travel on this thread into the unknown, hand in hand, moving upward.'

'How far, Mother? Did it seem a long way?'

'No, there wasn't any sense of time nor distance. It was another world, timeless, measureless, but not without direction. I definitely felt we were going up. We emerged into another environment. I can't explain it, too well. It was so different from anything we know here. I can only say what it was like. I'd compare it to a vast parkland; the most beautiful, restful, green park you can imagine. As far as I could see there extended this peaceful, restful scene of hills, soft as green velvet. They looked like they were carpeted, not with grass, but with some different element unknown to us.'

I could see my Mother was finding it hard to explain her experience. 'You rest a while. I'll get you a cup of coffee.'

'Do you want to stop now?' I asked as I handed her the cup. I wondered if this attempt to describe her wonderful revelation was reducing it to a distorted image.

'No, I want to share this with you, Jean. Then I don't want to ever talk about it again. It is too sacred. You may tell others whenever you feel it might glorify the Lord, but don't ask me to. I don't feel I can, somehow.'

As she sipped her coffee, I asked, 'What else was there that was so different than things are here?'

'The music,' she smiled. Her face was radiant just remembering it. 'The music was everywhere. I breathed it, like air. The atmosphere in that place was music. I was surrounded by it. I didn't see musicians, but sound seemed to take form in colour. Pastel colours blended and changed as the music varied in volume. It sounded similar to an orchestra and organ combined, and the moving colours were all one with it. It was above me, beneath me, moving through me.'

'Were there no other people there?' I asked.

'Oh yes, everywhere.'

'What were they doing? Sleeping?'

'Oh no, they were awake and moving around, but all seemed so relaxed and restful. Some were reclining.'

She remembered the names of many whom she recognised. She told me unusual names of people whom she had never known. I thought they sounded like Bible names. So I hurried to get the Bible with a proper name concordance. We found their names and texts in the Old and New Testaments that spoke of their faith in the Lord. I was surprised, since I knew that Mother had little Bible knowledge.

'Yes,' she said, 'I knew everyone whether I had met them before or not.' Then, leaning forward, she took my hand

and said, 'and the most wonderful thing of all is that I recognised my Mother.'

I gasped. How could that be true? Grandmother had died shortly after my Mother was born. There had been no way for her to remember her likeness. Yet, she described her features: the long black hair, the high cheekbones, the wide-set dark brown eyes. My grandmother was half American Indian and half Irish.

'It sounds like she had a strong Indian likeness,' I said.

'Do you remember your cousin Leonard?' she asked. He was the one we called 'the Indian' in our family because of his black hair and high cheekbones. 'Well, he looks a lot like your grandmother.'

'How can you be so sure, Mother?' I asked.

'I don't know, but I am as sure of that as I am that we are sitting here. I know I saw my mother in heaven.'

'How about your dad? You haven't mentioned him.'

A strange look passed over her face. 'No, and you know, until you asked me just now, I didn't realise that I didn't see him. There just didn't seem to be any memory of him at all. It's strange, I felt no loss at not seeing him there. Nothing.' Mother leaned back and looked out of the window a moment. 'Then, darling, as I stood there with Jesus, surrounded with the sights and sounds of heaven, I heard a voice penetrating it all. It was your voice.' She turned to look at me. I remembered that night when she first opened her eyes and asked me, 'Why did you bring me back?'

'Your voice was clear, insistent. I heard you cry, "Oh, Jesus, bring my mother back to me.' Jesus looked at me and said, "Grace, I will have to take you back." He took my hand and together we left that wonderful place, traveling down that thread of light. He let go of my hand and I felt myself settling into this tired body again. It was strange how I became aware of my earthly surrounding in several definite stages of restoration. First, my hearing. I could hear you praying and weeping before I could see you or speak to you. Next I could open my eyes and finally, I could speak.'

The music of heaven wafted into my mother's earthly consciousness several times afterwards. She would stop whatever she was doing and lift her head, enchanted, as she listened to music we could not hear.

'It seems like a breeze from another world brings it to me occasionally,' she explained. 'You know, Jean, heaven is not very far away. It is only a different dimension. It is so near that if our eyes and ears were only touched by God we could see it and hear it right now.'

I wondered, was this experience a vision, a dream? Was my mother actually in Paradise with Jesus? Did she see her mother, really see her? She seemed so sure, even describing her resemblance to my cousin Leonard.

A few months later a tangible object was placed into our hands that established the reality of it all.

Mother had fully recovered. Her heart suffered no lasting damage. She was so well we were able to visit relatives in West Virginia. Far back in the mountains we visited the old family farm. My grandmother's elder sister lived there. Aunt Sis, as she was called, had been dying in regal style for several years. A tiny, frail figure, she was propped against enormous white pillows trimmed in wide hand-crocheted lace. She ruled from her four-postered throne of feather ticks and reigned over a large, grown-up family that waited on her hand and foot. She shook her head and wept as we told her how Christ had changed our lives, rejoicing that her prayers had been answered.

As we stood around the bed, she beckoned to one of the family to hand her some things out of the old trunk near the bed. She said to my mother, 'Grace, here are some things that belonged to your mother. They were stored in this trunk before you were born. They should be yours. I want you to have them.'

We all stretched to see. Out of the trunk came a stack of old-fashioned crochet work, delicate lace and embroidery. Mother began to sort out each piece, almost caressing them. Her fingers touched something hard that slipped out from the folded fancy work. It was an old tintype photograph of a family. Mother pointed to a young woman in the group, exclaiming, 'There's my mother. Yes, that is my mother!'

'Grace,' said Aunt Sis, amazed, 'how could you know that? She died while holding you to her breast three days after you were born. You couldn't remember what she looked like. As far as I know, that was the only picture ever taken of her. An old traveling photographer, like a tinker, came along one day. I suppose she was only nineteen years old then.'

Mother was staring at the photo. 'I know her, for this is the beautiful girl I saw in heaven. Look Jean...' She held it up for me to see.

There she was, and she did look like Leonard.

CHAPTER FIVE

GOOD NEWS
TO THE POOR

'Will you go?' I was on my knees beside my bed. My Bible lay beside me, on the braided rag rug. I leaned against the soft bed covered with its patchwork quilt. As softly as the summer breeze that gently stirred the white lace curtains at my window, the Voice spoke again, 'Will you go for me?'

'Oh, yes, Jesus.' I knew he was asking me to be his missionary. 'Yes, yes, Lord,' I said with all the eagerness of a fifteen year old. 'I'll go anywhere for you.' Anywhere? Suddenly all the vivid missionary stories that Mrs. Keyes, my Methodist Sunday school teacher, had ever told me when I was a child flooded into my mind. She had included some vivid details of some of their sufferings. I waited and wept as the Lord showed me that I wasn't nearly wise enough nor strong enough to ever make such a big promise to him so glibly. 'Forgive me,' I repented. 'If you go with me, I'll go anywhere!'

Then he spoke to me from his Word.

'The Spirit of the Lord is upon me, because he has anointed me to preach good news to the poor. He has sent me to proclaim release to the captives and recovering of sight to the blind, to set at liberty those who are oppressed, to proclaim the acceptable year of the Lord' (Luke 4:18, 19).

'As the Father has sent me, even so I send you' (John 20:21).

I was conscious of a clear course to follow. A sense of direction was fixed in my soul. Before me lay the road of life: much of it hidden, obscure, but my destination was clear, a full view certainty...Heaven was ahead. Its gates were open, Jesus was there. Stretched between me and that glorious goal was a life-time of service in the Lord's harvest fields.

Heaven would have to wait. I knew now what I wanted more than anything else, even more than heaven itself. I looked up, kneeling by my bed, tears streaming down my face. 'Oh Jesus, here's my life. Add to it or take from it what you will, only there is just one thing I would ask, dear Lord. Please, when I have finished my life's work in your fields, let me meet you with my arms laden down with golden sheaves. Oh, don't let me meet you empty handed. Give me, dear Lord, precious souls for my hire. When I reach heaven, however long that may take, give me the joy of bringing many others with me.'

A few days later, I was telling our pastor all about my call as we enjoyed one of my mother's wonderful chicken dinners. Every Sunday our new pastor and his wife came for dinner. The evangelist, Mrs. Dalrymple, had gone on to other cities to minister. I was usually full of questions. As I studied my Bible during the week, I'd write down all the

things I didn't understand. Then, in those Sunday afternoon visits I'd get my answers. The Rev. William Allan paid
for those chicken dinners in full. He was my teacher, under
the blessed Holy Spirit. He taught me the Word, he taught
me how to pray and he taught me how to preach. In our
local church, he began leading me into this wonderful calling.

It wasn't long before I was preaching not only in our
local area, but farther from my home in Toledo, Ohio. The
next summer my parents returned to West Virginia for a
holiday in the mountains. They were telling all their relatives about the new life they had found in Christ. Daddy's
good health was an undeniable testimony to them. They
knew how he had been like a walking dead man for years.
They knew, too, that I had been desperately ill with dis-
eased kidneys. Their relatives listened as Dad and Mother
told them of the miracles that had happened to us and to so
many of our friends.

While visiting at one of the farms, some of the family
found out that I had done some preaching. 'Why don't we
arrange some services for Jean in the Union Church up on
the hill?' they suggested. 'We only have one church back
here in the hills for everybody; The Methodists, Baptists,
everybody comes.' Knowing how few of them ever attended
church, I thought it might be a good opportunity for some
practice on a small congregation. I agreed to stay, but my
Mother and Dad had to make the 500-mile trip back to
Ohio. The restaurant couldn't get along without Mother.

After my parents drove away, I walked up to the top of
the hill from my aunt's farmhouse to look at the church. It
wasn't as small as I'd expected! It seated at least four hundred. The pine walls glistened as the afternoon sun struck
the varnish. There was a row of oil lamps along each side of

the sanctuary. The pews were polished and a rustic beauty glistened in every part. Then I saw the big oak pulpit and began to laugh. I was short, how would they ever see me from behind that mammoth piece of furniture?

The evening of the first service, I left the farm early in order to pray in the church before others came. My pastor taught me to do that. While I prayed behind the huge pulpit, I could hear the sounds of people entering. Several times it seemed I could hear lots of people coming in cars and parking them. I glanced at my watch. It was time to start. I wondered why no one had come up to speak to me about the order of the service. I stood up, peeking tentatively over the pulpit. I gasped and dropped to my knees again, hiding behind it. The place was packed!

I was sixteen and now I really was on my own. There was no pastor, no song leader, no organist! 'Isn't there anyone to lead the singing?' I asked. A bald man on the front row wearing silver-rimmed spectacles timidly arose. Several people nodded their heads as if to assure me that he was the right man for the job. 'Would you like to start?' I suggested. He fumbled in his pocket. 'Whatever is he doing?' I thought. He extracted a small metal object, held it up, gently struck it and he and several people hummed in harmony with its single note. It was the first time I had ever seen a tuning fork! It was the first time, also, that I had heard a group of selected 'singers' sing in one corner of the church while the rest sat looking on as if they were being tested for their deafness!

'O-o-on Jordan's stormy bands I stand, A-a-and cast a wishful eye…' their voices painfully wailed.

'Oh Lord, what am I going to do?' I prayed. I realised there was little to do that night, but much to do before the next night.

'Uncle Jesse,' I was talking to him on the telephone long distance, 'can you come and help me? I've some meetings here in Coolridge and there's no organist. There is an organ.' I didn't tell him it was out of tune and as old as the hills! Uncle Jesse was one of the finest musicians in Charleston, West Virginia and a piano tuner as well. He was just the man I needed, except for one thing. He was scarcely ever sober. 'You'll have to promise me that you'll stay sober for three weeks, Uncle Jesse.' I prayed as I waited for his answer. It was hard for him to say 'no'—I was his favourite niece. 'Well, Jean,' he drawled, 'I wouldn't do it for anyone else but you!'

Soon the organ was repaired I prayed for Uncle Jesse, knowing there were moonshine stills all around him. He played the old hymns with the joy of a new convert. He had never been so close to the altar!

In the evenings, while I was preaching, I often heard a noise like air hissing out of an inner tube. It took awhile before I identified it. It was coming from an area where a large black, pot-bellied stove sat. The nights in the mountains were chilly and damp. People were cold after walking so far. By the time the services started, the stove was red hot, its bulging sides glowing like a candied apple. Those who sat nearby had opened the door of the stove. 'Hiss-s-s-s-s!' 'Hiss-s-s-s-s!' I looked over just in time to see that a group of old ladies on the front row, chewing tobacco, were spitting with dead-eye accuracy out of the corners of their mouths into the hot coals.

Another thing I noticed was that some of the congregation didn't speak to each other and, moreover, sat in separate sections which appeared to be 'off limits' to any other groups. These were the 'hard-shelled' Baptists as opposed to the Methodists, and so it went on all around the church.

They were in a Union Church but they were not united! So, it was among these poor, divided, rather cheerless worshipers that God sent me to preach the gospel.

Soon, the Holy Spirit began to convict of sin. People began to repent, confess and forgive one another. Then I announced, 'Tomorrow night there will be prayer for the sick.' Everyone looked surprised. It was probably the first time a divine healing service had ever been held there. They looked uneasily at each other, but after the service that night no one said anything to me about my announcement.

When I arrived the next evening, I thought that maybe I was late, The place was full and there was still an hour before the service was due to start. The word had spread like wildfire through the hills. They had come from far and near to see what this sixteen-year-old girl hoped to do that night! I reminded the Lord when I knelt behind the big old pulpit that He had sent me to preach the gospel and to heal the sick. How I longed for my pastor. I needed someone. I glanced at Uncle Jesse. He smiled back, holding up his thumb. It was a signal that he was sober and ready to start.

After my sermon I called for those who were sick to come forward. Every seat was full. People were standing inside and outside. Many were looking through the windows. They started moving around allowing the sick to come. They filled the altar space, they filled the middle aisle and still they were pressing in. We sang, 'Only believe, only believe. All things are possible, only believe.'

'I want you all to pray with me,' I said, meaning it fervently, as I called the sick to form a line at the front. It seemed as though the audience were spectators at an exhibition, rather than a congregation of prayerful believers. For most of them this was something they had never been to before and they weren't about close their eyes and miss it!

'What is your affliction?' I asked the tall, lanky boy dressed in denim overalls. He stared down at me. He was around six foot three and I was scarcely five feet tall. I asked again, raising my voice a little, 'What is your affliction?' No answer. He just stared at me, looking bewildered. Suddenly a little grandma with a tight 'hallelujah knot' of greying hair on the back of her head, shot around from behind him and piped, 'He was born deaf.'

'Oh, Lord,' I inwardly groaned, 'couldn't you have given me someone with stomach trouble first?'

'He can't talk either,' his grandmother added.

I remembered how I had seen my pastor place his fingers in deaf people's ears and pray for them. I had read in the Bible how Jesus had done this, too. So, stretching up on tip-toe, I placed my fingers in his ears and said, 'In the name of Jesus receive your hearing.' Everyone was looking, some standing up to see. I waited. He glanced around nervously, and suddenly clamped his hands over both ears. A look of pain crossed his face.

'Stop playing the organ, Uncle Jesse,' I said. He had been playing softly, trying to lend a little more reverence to the scene. I realised that the boy could hear for the first time. Softly I said, 'Say "Jesus".' He tried, but his voice was high and screechy like the sound of a bow drawn across a violin string. 'Jesus,' I repeated, until he was able to modulate his voice to a normal pitch. He was hearing and speaking. I don't believe I've ever heard the name of Jesus spoken more beautifully.

Hearts were melted and faces glowed with joy. Faith streaked down the rest of the waiting line like lightning across a summer evening sky. They were no longer an audience, but a congregation gathering closer to Jesus and to one another. Many were healed before they ever reached the front where I stood praying. It was after midnight when the last flickering oil lamp was blown out.

The remaining days of the three week revival meeting were overflowing with singing and laughter and excitement. Dad and Mother came back for me on the day of my last service. When we finally were able to tear ourselves away from the grateful people whom we had learned to love so much, we started to get into the car. Dad stopped and called out, 'Hey! Come and look at this!' It looked like a truck loaded for the market. There were burlap bags of potatoes, carrots and onions; baskets of eggs, fresh dressed chickens; bags of green beans, tomatoes, corn on the cob, and smooth round balls of golden butter. Gleaming jars of strawberry preserves, tomato preserves and apple butter were neatly packed in boxes. There was hardly a place for me to sit! We stared in amazement. Men, women and children crowded around the car, happy to see our surprise. One of the farmers, who was custodian and acted as preacher when no one else was around, smiled shyly. 'We're sorry we couldn't give you a love offering of money. The coal mine is shut down and some of us haven't much cash around. We thought maybe you could take this and use it. It's not much, I suppose, but it's all we got. We wanted to give you something.' He glanced at my mother and said, 'We're sure glad you let her come!'

It was my first love offering. No other would ever have more love in it.

CHAPTER SIX

HE HAS SENT ME

The train moved slowly out of the Toledo Railway Station, as if reluctant to separate us. Blinking back the tears and smiling bravely, Mother and Dad waved good-bye. There was a hard jerk and the train rolled faster around the curve until my parents were out of sight. I was on my way to California to attend LIFE Bible College. Beside me rested a carefully packed lunch that was to last me until I arrived in Los Angeles three days later. In my purse was scarcely more than my train ticket.

Since our conversions, Mother's restaurant business had declined. Previously there had been a bar, slot machines and other extra attractions that drew a certain kind of trade that liked a little fun with their meals. The dance floor and banqueting rooms had been scenes of some pretty wild parties. When these began to go the trade had dropped off. So it was for several practical reasons, as well as with good spiritual wisdom, that Mother advised me to earn my own money to go to the Bible College. 'If you're going into a ministry that depends on faith, then you might just as well start now at this end. You'll appreciate your trip and studies there if you have to pray and work for your expenses.'

It was a good challenge and I accepted it. In fact, I decided not to work for my mother in the restaurant, as I had been doing, but to get a job elsewhere. It was in a spice packing factory. It was hard work among foreign women who smelled stronger, swore harder and laughed louder than most men I'd met. They were rough and suspicious of newcomers like myself. It was good training for someone who was usually surrounded by friendly, smiling Christians and congenial customers. Some evenings when I walked out from under the silent, stony glares of the women in the factory, I vowed never to go back, but I'd return the next day, determined not to give up. It wasn't like I'd be there the rest of my life. I had a goal ahead. In time I came to realise that the loud laughter and hard swearing were a cover up for a lot of problems in those women's lives. They never showed that they liked me much, but during the lunch breaks, they seemed quite interested to hear what the Lord had done for us. I found out, too, why they smelled strongly—I soon smelled just like them! I especially had sympathy with them after I had been packing garlic all day. It was fun going home on the bus, watching passengers switch seats like musical chairs to get away from me.

Soon I had enough money saved for the ticket, and I didn't wait a day longer than I needed to. 'But you need money for your expenses on the way and after you get there. It may be a while before you get work,' Mother protested.

'I'll go by faith and trust that the Lord will take care of that at the other end. He can't do it until I get there. I've got to go.' So I had the faith and Mother packed the lunch.

The day I arrived in Los Angeles, I had one hard boiled egg left. I'd been eating fried chicken most of the way. Thirty-eight cents rattled in my purse. Someone told me that I could get a street car that would take me right to the doors of Angelus Temple. I wasn't worried, until I stepped off the train. The Los Angeles station was packed with people. It seemed as though I was plunged into a sea of strangers and I was in danger of being swallowed up and completely lost in this huge, unfamiliar city. Struggling to regain my sense of direction and to get my goal in sight, I moved along with the hundreds of others who swarmed towards the exits. On either side of me, behind ropes that formed the corridor, crowds of people were waiting. I looked, hoping for a smile even from a stranger. 'I wonder where the street car stop is.' I thought. Suddenly I heard my name, 'Jean! Jean!' I hesitated, glanced around and hurried on, feeling for sure no one would know me. 'Besides there must be lots of Jeans around here,' I thought, and laughed inwardly at the pun.

'Jean! Jean Murphy!'

'Wait! There can't be many Jean Murphys around here,' I realised. Two people on the side were leaning over the rope, waving and laughing at my look of surprise. 'Hi! We've been waiting for you. We were hoping you'd be here.'

I recognised one of them. She was Audrey, a girl whom I'd met at a youth camp in Ohio. We'd talked together about our dreams of going to college in Los Angeles. She was through with her high school and was planning to go that autumn. I planned to go in the autumn, too. 'Send in your application with mine and I'll be there to meet you when you come,' she had said. 'Great,' I had replied excitedly. The application was sent and accepted but it was February when I finally came walking through that station. I hadn't written to say when I was arriving, so of course I wasn't expecting to be met by Audrey—and who was this other person? 'Jean, this is Mildred Holcomb, the registrar at our college.' We exchanged greetings. 'Here, let's take your baggage checks and get out of this mob,' Audrey said. 'The car's right over here.'

Parked by the station was a red convertible. As I rode in style past the clanging street car, I praised the Lord that I still had my thirty-eight cents. 'How did you happen to come down here today?' I couldn't hold the question back any longer.

Audrey looked over her shoulder from the front seat. 'Well, this morning when I came into college, Mildred asked me if I knew when you were coming. I said I didn't, since your plans had changed.'

'Let me explain,' Mildred broke in as she drove. ' When I was waiting on the Lord this morning, your name came to me. It was rather surprising, for I suppose there must be dozens of names of prospective students who have changed their arrival dates. Yet I couldn't stop thinking "Jean Murphy" all the way to the office. I checked the files and I saw that you were supposed to come last September. There was no note giving a new date of arrival, so I decided to check with Audrey.'

Audrey turned in her seat to look at me. 'Mildred said, "Let's go down and meet the Challenger train at eleven o'clock. I feel strongly that Jean will be on that train!" You can imagine how surprised I was!' Audrey said.

'No more surprised than I.' My heart beat fast with excitement.

'Shut your eyes, Jean,' Audrey suddenly told me. 'Don't open them until I tell you to.' The car slowed down. I could tell it was making a turn around a corner. 'Now look!' Before me was a dream come true, a picture come alive, a vision fulfilled. A placid lake surrounded by sentinel palm trees, verdant lawns and gardens, lay before me. At the far end, beyond the willows, rising above the cypress, I saw scintillating in the southern California sunshine spacious Angelus Temple. Beside it stood LIFE Bible College. The domed temple, home of the Church of the Foursquare Gospel, was pastored by Aimee Semple Mcpherson, the smiling lady on the front of the old Bridal Call magazine that Bumbang had found in her brother's trunk!

By three o'clock that afternoon, I had a good job in a Los Angeles bank.

During the first week, I got settled in the dormitory, met lots of students, enrolled in the College, and attended a service in Angelus Temple. It was the graduation of the Pathfinders class from LIFE college. I was excited, staring like a typical tourist, sitting in that great auditorium. I'd been told it was the world's largest Protestant church, seating five thousand. I couldn't take my eyes away from the eight stained glass windows. They glowed with colourful scenes of the Saviour's life. I looked up at the balconies and on up to the vast sky-like dome.

What a contrast, sitting here with these thousands of worshippers, to the little store-front church in Toledo, Ohio. The only thing in Angelus Temple that was anything like our church at home was the text on the arch above the wide platform. The letters were larger and more elaborate, but they said the same thing: "Jesus Christ, the same yesterday and today and forever."

I felt someone jabbing me with her elbow. Vona, my new roommate, was pointing towards the platform.

'Jean, look here, quick.'

'What? Look at what?' I said, straining to see the platform full of robed graduates and faculty.

'Not what...who,' she corrected me. 'See that young man coming to the pulpit? He's valedictorian of his class. He's going to speak.'

I nodded, finding it hard to keep my eyes on any one person.

'Well, that is Elmer Darnall. I know him. He is from Des Moines, Iowa. You ought to meet him. He'd be nice for you.'

Vona, like others in the dorm, enjoyed trying to pair off students who would make likely partners in the marrying game.

'You know, I think you and Elmer Darnall would really hit it off.' She looked at me and grinned.

I wasn't interested. There were plenty of things much more important to me during the coming weeks. Being a joiner, it was not long before I was involved in all kinds of extra activities on top of my regular studies. For months I worked during the day, attended classes at night and every weekend was full of action. I roared along at a superhuman rate until suddenly, I dropped, literally, in the hall of the dorm, unconscious. When I opened my eyes, a kindly Christian doctor informed me that I must remain completely quiet—no visitors, no final exams, nothing for several weeks, in fact for the whole summer! 'Impossible', I thought. The whole thing should never have happened and I wasn't about it take it lying down. When I started to get out of bed, I couldn't move! I had never felt so frustrated. 'You have had a nervous collapse and you'll have to rest,' the doctor said firmly.

A nurse, who seemed more like a warden than a nurse to me, was posted. Actually, she was a gift from God to help me to endure the long weeks that followed.

Inwardly, I was raging. Why did this have to happen? I was mad at myself and the devil, and if not slightly peeved with God, I was certainly perplexed. I thought things like this shouldn't happen to Christians. Frustrations burned inside me for weeks until I finally sank into the bleak, black ashes of despair. I thought I was a failure, finished. Then the Holy Spirit sent me a teacher. I had a lot to learn that couldn't be taught in a textbook. It was a short lesson with a long-lasting effect. Mildred Holcomb, the one whom the Lord had sent to meet me at the train, came to my bedside. I was too weak to say much to her. She put a finger to her lips signaling for me to be still. After a long silence, she said softly, 'I want to share a secret with you, Jean. It's in Colossians 1:27— "Christ in you, the hope of glory".' She took my hand. 'Jean, Christ in you…He is your sufficiency. "You are complete in him."'–Colossians 2:10. She seemed about to say more, then hesitated as if she had been checked. She squeezed my hand, smiled and whispered good-bye. I was alone in a silent room with the secret, 'Christ in you, the hope of glory.'

How hopeless I felt as I lay there! I was drained, empty. All my unfinished plans and projects tormented me, demanding my attention and condemning me for not being stronger, wiser and more efficient. Accusations were filling my mind most of the time. Futility flooded my whole being, leaving me limp with weakness. I was crushed, squeezed out. There was nothing left in me. I could never work hard again. 'I have nothing more to give to anything or anyone— not even to you, Lord,' I inwardly lamented. 'Christ in you.' The words pushed themselves into my thoughts.

'Oh, Lord, where are you?'

'I will never leave you. I am with you, Jean.'

'What's wrong with me, Lord?'

'I want you to abide in me as I abide in you. You offer me your efforts, your service, your time. I want you, Jean, not your gifts. I've given myself to you, now give yourself to me. Talk to me, love me and enjoy my presence.'

Memories of the night I had knelt at the altar in the little church in Toledo came back to me. How vain and proud I had been, coming to Jesus with my offer of a fair deal - my 'one good turn deserves another' attitude. Works, that's all I ever seemed to give him. Self-effort was my currency to pay God back for his blessings. Right from the beginning I had tried to give him my sins instead of myself, the sinner. The night I came to Christ I had been told that if I only confessed my sins, he would forgive them, but if I yielded my entire self to him, he would thoroughly cleanse me and change me for his glory.

I remembered when he called me into the ministry, I had been so quick to accept the call, full of self-confidence. He had shown me that enthusiasm was not enough, and had patiently waited until I admitted that without him I could do nothing.

Now here I was again, trying even harder than ever to please him. 'Don't try, Jean, trust. Not aggression but submission. Come near to me. I am waiting for your fellowship. Believe that I am in you and you are in me.'

'But all this work there is to do,' I protested.

'Leave the work - you can't do it, but you can worship me and I'll do the work in you and through you.'

I turned my thoughts away from all the things I couldn't do and did that which I was still able to do. Weak as I was, I worshipped Jesus. Then I knew I wasn't alone, nor empty. For several days I sensed the glory of his presence flowing over me. It seemed I had been away and had just come back and it was good! I was elated, accepted and loved. He restored my soul and renewed the joy of my salvation.

CHAPTER SEVEN

WHOEVER
DOES NOT DOUBT

My roommate dashed up the stairs of the girls' dorm. Bursting into our room she blurted out, "He's coming. I saw him. He's coming up the street.' She was dragging me out on to the upstairs porch.

'Wait a minute,' I protested. "Who's coming? What're you talking about?'

'Remember that Elmer Darnall I told you about? Well, he's been in the eastern states preaching and he's back,' she panted. ' Look he's coming up the street. I saw him and hurried back to tell you,' she said proudly.

I couldn't keep from looking, although I didn't want her nor the other girls who were coming out on the porch to think I was too curious.

'You've got to meet him,' Vona whispered as the unsuspecting, serious looking young man strolled by. "I'll see to it,' she added. We all giggled.

Elmer came back from the east to do post-graduate work and to produce a series of radio dramatisations of Bible stories at United Artists studios. A few days after Vona's promise, 'I'll see to it', Elmer sent a note asking me to take a part in a radio play. He'd heard me speak, he wrote, and thought my voice would be perfect. I was flattered, but cautious.

The recording sessions lengthened into all-day dates and before long we realised that we had more than an average interest in each other. I was on guard, though. The Lord had helped me to sort out my priorities and I didn't want anything, nor anyone to come between me and the Lord. Besides, there was something else that had happened. God had given me a definite call to Panama.

Echo Park Lake, across from Angelus Temple, was off bounds to students at night. During the day, however, it was a sunny campus and an ideal spot for dating couples. Since Elmer and I both worked nights at Lockheed Aircraft, and attended college day classes, our dates were in the afternoons. Because of the little time we had, we'd often dash across the street and hire a boat. One afternoon, in a secluded inlet of the lake, we talked about our future. We discovered that God had given us the same calling to the Spanish speaking people. Fears of our relationship not being in God's will vanished—We accepted the love and calling that was to make us one.

After a short engagement, we were married in Angelus Temple. Aimee Semple McPherson, our pastor and teacher officiated and blessed our marriage. We began the adventure of a united commitment; an adventure that soon took us to the Republic of Panama. Suddenly, married life meant missionary life. Our adventure was to adapt, not only to each other, but to a Latin culture, a tropical climate and a strange language. We also shared the joy of life-bearing, the birth of our son, but not before we experienced together the sorrow of our first-born's death in Panama. 'Why, why?' my heart insisted upon asking in the Balboa hospital. Then a voice as clear as a friend's spoke. 'Faith doesn't ask why.' I was speechless, subdued, surrounded, in the solemn stillness of the Lord's presence. Elmer and I learned during the days that followed much more of the meaning of those words We discovered the faith which works by love.

A year later, John, our son, was born in a Canal Zone hospital in Panama. When the time came for us to return to the interior, I took him back to the hospital for a checkup. The doctor's face changed as he examined the baby. 'This child has one of the worst attacks of asthma I have ever seen in an infant,' he told us.

'It must be a cold,' I argued. Although asthma, hay fever and exzema were on both sides of our family, I couldn't accept the doctor's diagnosis. Elmer and I had expressly prayed before John's birth that he would not have any allergies.

'No, it's asthma,' the doctor insisted. 'You'll have to watch him. He'll probably never be too active in sports or things like that later on.'

By the time we got back to our little house on stilts, we knew it was asthma, too. The baby sounded like a wheezing steam calliope. There wasn't a room in the house where you couldn't hear him pulling for breath as he lay on our bed. It was agony for us all. Dropping to our knees in desperation, we cried out to the Lord. As we prayed, desperation gave way to affirmation. We began to thank him that he had heard us. The attack wore on, sounding worse by the minute, but our faith seemed to be strengthened as we prayed in the Spirit for our child.

There was another reason why we were so sure that John would not be weak and handicapped with asthma. Six weeks before his birth, doctors had informed Elmer that our child would be stillborn. 'There is no longer a heart-beat,' they said. Elmer went from the hospital down to the beach and cried. It was a hard time for him. There were problems all around him stemming from difficulties that always seem to be magnified on the mission field. This was almost more than he could bear. Walking back and forth in the middle of the dark night, it seemed discouragement was pounding inside him like the surf upon the sand. Then the Lord's words came to him, 'Truly, I say to you, whoever does not doubt in his heart, but believes that what he says will come to pass, it will be dome for him,' (Mark 11:23). Then a quietness, deep and powerful, settled the storm and Elmer heard himself saying, 'This baby will live. It will be a well, strong baby.' He repeated the words again and again until he was fairly singing them. He knew the baby would live and be strong.

'This baby shall be well and strong,' we agreed as we knelt beside the bed. We praised God by faith, assured in our hearts that he would be faithful to perform that which he had promised. Time was forgotten as the hours passed by. Suddenly, we realised that we were praising the Lord without the accompaniment of Johnny's wheezing. He was fast asleep! He was healed and never had asthma again.

A similar crisis occurred when La Donna was born eight years later. We had returned from Panama and were preparing to go to Australia. When we realised a baby was on the way, I found it hard to understand the Lord's timing. When I prayed, he assured me that this baby girl he was giving us would be a source of sunshine to us all our lives. I couldn't reject a prospect like that! It was grim, though.

We were on an itinerary that extended from the west coast of the United States to eastern Canada. Elmer and I took turns speaking every night in a different town. By the end of four months we agreed that I should stay at my mother's while Elmer finished the tour.

When I arrived home, I was shocked to find my dad bedfast with multiple sclerosis. Two days later, my mother was brought home badly injured from an accident in the factory where she worked. Being pregnant and exhausted, I didn't seem to be much help. Gloom settled on the place like a black cloud.

A group of Mother's Mormon relatives came to visit us at that time and they found it hard to understand our kind of Christianity that would take me and my husband to the other side of the world when my dad was dying and my mother's arm was injured. It didn't look good. I went upstairs to talk it over with my dad. He lay pale and thin under the brightly coloured patchwork quilt my mother had made years ago. I remembered the same quilt on my bed the night I had wept by my bedside and said, 'If Jesus goes with me, I'll go anywhere.' The blinds were drawn and the room was full of soft shadows.

I took Dad's hand in mine. Dad, I want to talk about something with you.' He nodded. 'We really do feel it is God's will for us to go. That's the only reason we would want to leave at a time like this, but Aunt Clara and the other relatives downstairs don't think we're fair to leave you both like this. Maybe they're right.' I waited to see if Dad had anything to say. He looked at me with tears in his blue eyes. 'I was wondering…if you say so, Dad, we'll stay and wait for you and mother to get better. The Bible says to honour your father and mother. After all, I am your daughter and I was your daughter before I became a Christian. It seems my first duty is to you.'

'Jean,' Dad stopped me. 'Jean, I want you and Elmer to be in God's will. You'll do your mother and me more good by being in God's will than by staying here. I need your prayers. I want God to answer those prayers. You don't get answers when you're outside his will. You and Elmer go on. God will take care of us.' Suddenly he seemed to have new strength and gripped my hand with the power of faith. We make our covenant with God.

One of the happiest moments of my life was when I saw our little newborn girl. Yet, within a few hours, I was to be plunged into a pit of fear. I had suffered extremely with gall stones before she was born. For weeks I had scarcely been able to drink or eat anything. Several hours after her birth, a slow, seeping darkness seemed to come over me. Down, down I was sinking. I struggled for the bell and as I pressed it, I went unconscious. I came to with a sharp jab of pain in my back. A spinal fluid test was being taken to see why I was paralysed on my whole right side. I had suffered a stroke! I heard someone mention polio and fear flooded in. What would become of my baby? When Elmer came In several hours later with flowers and chocolates for me, he was amazed to hear me try to say out of the side of my twisted face, 'I've got polio.' The words were slurred, but he got the message. He ran for the doctor. I could hear the nurse trying to calm him down. 'Rev. Darnall, we aren't sure if it's polio or not, but your wife is very ill.'

People began to pray in several churches in Toledo. Nurses watched and doctors kept checking to see where the blood clot that had caused my stroke might have lodged. Elmer and I began to realise that all of this was not just a coincidence of extraordinary problems all hitting at once. This was an all-out attack. We could trace it back to the time we had definitely made our plans to go to Australia. The devil didn't like it. He struck left, right and center. Dad's illness, Mother's accident, my stroke all added up to demonic resistance springing from every side. 'It can only mean that God is going to do something great in Australia,' Elmer said.

We took authority over the enemy in prayer and resisted him with praise and affirmation of faith in the power of Jesus' name. As I claimed the victory and told my doctor and nurses of our plans to go to Australia, my doctor became annoyed. 'Mrs. Darnall,' he said, 'if you go out of this hospital in a wheelchair, you'll be lucky, let alone travelling to Australia.' Overcoming faith soared, however, as the battle raged. Each day there was an obvious improvement. My sight, which had been double, cleared. My speech returned to normal as the paralysis left my face. My arm was restored to its full usefulness and finally if felt as though warm sand was running down my leg as new life flowed in. But it stopped at my ankle - my right foot was numb. When I asked a nurse to help me get up, she said, 'Mrs. Darnall, you must be careful, We're not sure yet about the blood clot. It could hit your heart, you know.'

I tried standing on my foot. It was like a block of wood. I couldn't walk without limping. 'Look, will you help me? I don't want to go back to this bed until I'm walking perfectly. I know that Jesus will not leave me like this. I want to walk by faith. Will you help me?' My tiny nurse was a nun from Spain. She looked like a Dresden doll, delicate and dainty, with huge, soft brown eyes. She glanced down the hall. 'All right, we shall try, just for a little while,'

"In the name of Jesus,' I kept repeating as I limped, dragging my lifeless foot along. 'In the name of Jesus,' she repeated with a voice like a chapel bell. In the name of Jesus we walked backwards and forwards, pausing to praise Him at each end of the hall. After a time it felt as if a sluice gate had opened. Life poured into my foot. I was released completely.

I walked into my room praising God. The little nun ran down the hall to the Mother in charge of the ward. 'Come quickly and see what the name of Jesus has done,' I heard her shout. The older nun came running in. As she watched me walking and praising God, she took hold of the silver cross at her waist and said, 'Mrs. Darnall, you'd make a wonderful Catholic!' I laughed and replied, 'You'd make a wonderful Protestant!' We both laughed and praised the name of our Lord together.

When we brought the new baby home, there was a mixture of joy and sorrow. Mother was so pleased and Johnny was delighted to welcome his new sister, but Dad didn't recognise me. His mind was affected by his illness. He pushed the baby away. We were like strangers to him.

The day came when we had to go on with our journey towards Australia. The first stage was Los Angeles. From there we would sail to the land 'down under'. The moment we had all dreaded came. We were gathered at the open door of our home in Toledo. Red hollyhocks were blooming around the doorway. The traffic roared past as we waited for the taxi that would take us to the train. We couldn't say good-bye to Dad. It was no use. He didn't understand a word. He lay sleeping upstairs. Mother stood holding the baby with her good arm. Johnny, sensing the tension of the moment, stood clutching his grandma's apron, looking as though he was about to cry. Elmer glanced outside to see if the taxi was coming. 'Good-bye, Mother,' I said, searching her face for a sign of the courageous smile that always seemed to be there. She couldn't speak. 'You know it's only because we're sure it's right. We're sure it's God's will that we go, Mother. We couldn't stand to leave you otherwise.' I tried to explain.

"How can you be so sure?" she blurted out with pain in her voice. 'You keep saying that all these things have happened because the devil is trying to keep you from going. How do you know it isn't the Lord trying to save you from making some big mistake? How can you be sure that this is God's will?' Her words struck like cold, icy sleet. I couldn't answer She handed the baby over to me. 'It doesn't seem like God would take my two grandchildren away from me, and you two, when your father is so ill. I need you so much.'

'Mother!' I cried out.

'I can't help it,' she went on. 'I just can't accept this as God's will.' I was about to console her somehow with a word of comfort when Elmer said, 'Let's pray before we go, the taxi's coming.' As we prayed and wept together, I remembered Elmer's words in the hospital, 'It can only mean that God is going to do something great in Australia.'

In California there were last minute speaking engagements, and all the final arrangements such as visas, packing and injections. It was when our daughter, La Donna, was getting her shots that the doctor noticed she had a rash. He examined her more closely. There was inflammation around her eyes and infection in her ears. I'd like to make some tests on this rash, too. Are there any allergies in your family or your husband's?'

'On both sides,' I reluctantly admitted.

'I thought so. This looks like weeping eczema.'

Elmer and I prayed again, 'She's yours, Lord, and we praise you for the victory.' When we returned to the doctor's office, it wasn't necessary for the doctor to open the tear ducts. They were opened! The abscesses in her ears were healed, too. The news wasn't so bright regarding the eczema, though. The rash had spread and a watery substance was oozing from every inflamed area. We found that she was allergic to cow's milk, orange juice, eggs, flour and meat, and she couldn't wear anything with wool in it! 'All she can eat is soya milk, nothing else,' the doctor advised. 'I wouldn't take a baby with that problem to Australia, if I were you. How do you know you'll find a soya milk formula over there?'

We heard that the Bordan Company made a ready-to-use formula. We checked with them and were told that it could be secured in the same form in Australia. We took an ample supply of the formula for the trip. 'We probably won't need it when we reach there,' I said hopefully, but LaDonna was still allergic when we got there, and we needed more formula. Elmer went to clinics, hospitals, grocery stores and health shops all over Sydney. No one had ever heard of soya milk. Our stock was gone and the baby was ill. In despair Elmer said, 'If we don't find something soon, we'll have to go back to America.' We remembered mother's words, 'How can you be so sure it's God's will for you to go to Australia?' Then it happened. Elmer found the answer in a small delicatessen store in a quaint arcade. 'No, I don't have soya bean milk,' the manager said, 'but I do have soya flour and a recipe for a baby's formula.' Overjoyed, Elmer brought home a huge bag of flour, jars of honey and all the ingredients we needed. Quickly, we prepared it and, thank God, La Donna liked it!

As we continued our itinerary in Australia, every house we stayed in smelled like a soya bean factory. Fortunately, LaDonna thrived on her mixture and all our difficulties didn't hinder our ministry. As we travelled in eastern Australia, needy people answered to the claims of Christ, surrendered their lives to him and were healed. Many Christians were receiving the overflowing power of the Holy Spirit. God was doing great things in Australia!

One of the first letters from Mother sounded fairly encouraging. I could tell she was trying to be brave. 'Don't get your hopes up too high,' she wrote, 'but your Dad seems a little better.' The next letter informed us that he had asked what time it was that day. Before long, he was fully rational, sitting up and finally coming downstairs for his meals. Within five months of our arrival in Australia, he was back working full-time for the Kaiser Jeep Corporation. What a test of faith it had been. Mother had said, 'How can you be so sure it's God's will for you to go to Australia?' Dad had staked his life on it being God's will. Mother's arm healed, too, although there was a slight stiffness left in two fingers.

During those first months in Australia, I would thank the Lord for LaDonna's healing as I gave her the formula in a bottle. There were times when I'd tried to slip milk instead of soya formula into her bottle, but this only made her sick and small blisters would form where the milk happened to touch her skin.

One Sunday morning during a holy communion service in Perth, Western Australia, the Lord increased my faith. As I accepted the bread, I suddenly shared it with our nine-month-old daughter. I also let La Donna sip from the cup. Recognising the body and the blood of our Blessed Lord, I whispered, 'By His stripes you are healed.' Later at lunch, I told Mr. and Mrs. Britton, the friends with whom we were staying, what I had done during the communion service. Bunny Britton took a biscuit from the table and gave it to LaDonna. She held a cup of milk to the baby's mouth. 'Here, LaDonna, drink this.' Some of it spilled, dripping off her chin, as she drank. LaDonna wasn't sick. No blisters appeared on her face. Gurgling and smiling, she reached out for more. She was never allergic again.

CHAPTER EIGHT

BECAUSE HE
HAS ANOINTED ME

We sailed through a storm to get to Western Australia, but the sky was a brilliant blue when we disembarked at Fremantel harbour. It had been a rough passage from Adelaide across the Great Australian Bight. Johnny, our eight-year-old son, took a deep breath of the western air and said, 'This is just like being home.' For some inexplicable reason Elmer and I felt the same.

During the following weeks of gospel services in the Victoria Park Town Hall, many people answered the claims of the cross upon their lives. There were miracles of healing, so much so that the newspapers ran feature stories that brought people from all parts of the state to the services and an avalanche of mail. Soon there was a drawn-up request presented above a long list of signatures for us to remain and establish a church.

On the other side of the Nullarbor we had churches waiting for us to keep our commitment to them. For the first time in our ministry, Elmer and I strongly disagreed about which way to go. I felt we should fulfill our obligations to those whom we had promised future meetings. He felt drawn towards these happy, loving people who claimed they needed us so much. Inwardly, I was afraid that we would be misunderstood by other churches in the area and our reputation with established churches and pastors there and in other places would be damaged. The fear of losing our good name as evangelists filled my heart. 'What would they say?' crowded my mind. I wasn't even trying to hear what God said. We continued to disagree until finally I countered with a temporary compromise. 'I'll go early and finish up the itinerary we have there. You stay here and continue with the meetings. If by the time I've had the last meetings in eastern Australia, you still feel like staying here in Perth, I'll come back.'

'Oh no, we're in this together and so we'll either stay here or both go back east together. Compromise is just the devil's trick to get us apart.' Elmer waited for my decision. I was silent. Finally he said, 'I'll tell you what I'm willing to do. I'll go over to the bush'(a natural reserve of Australian bush that was just across from where we were staying) 'to fast and pray for three days. We'll know at the end of that time.'

'I know now,' I stubbornly insisted in my mind. Aloud I said, 'That's all right by me.' I felt he would have liked it better if I'd offered to fast and pray too. Dodging the danger of really hearing the Lord's voice on this, I kept busy after Elmer went across the road into the bush. On the second day I decided I'd go to town for a little shopping. I felt uneasy. My prayers had become unusually short and I was reading shorter psalms! Walking through the St. George's Arcade, I stopped to admire some lovely bone china in a gift shop window. A voice behind me asked, 'Aren't you Jean Darnall?'

I was startled and with a slight tone of impatience replied, 'Yes, why?'

I have a word for you from the Lord!' I felt cold, trying to think of an excuse to get away from this woman, whoever she was.

'You probably don't know me, although I've been in a number of your services, Mrs Darnall. I'm a member of a church here in the city and work with the Campaigners for Christ. This morning I was praying for you and felt very definitely that I must find you and tell you something.'

I interrupted. 'How did you find me?'

'I just asked the Lord to lead me and he led me here.' She looked at me with a big smile. I felt like weeping. 'Mrs Darnall, the Lord wants you and your husband to stay here in Perth. You're needed to raise up a standard for the full gospel. When you do, it'll draw many of the people who are scattered closer to one another and to the Lord.'

It seemed I was standing in the middle of a green field. Children were clumped together in every corner far apart from each other. Suddenly they began to run towards the centre of the field where I was standing by a huge maypole. They gathered up the flowered garlands that hung limply from the pole and began to dance with joy around and around in the sunshine. I stood under their canopy, listening to their laughter. As they came closer to the pole, they came closer to each other.

'...and so, Mrs Darnall, I just wanted you to know that many people in many churches would be very thankful if you and your husband would remain here. I'm sure the Lord would be pleased, too.'

I was mumbling some sort of a thank you with tears on my face, trying to get the words past the lump in my throat, when suddenly the messenger disappeared in the crowd of shoppers. I hurried down George Street to go home and find Elmer and to tell him!

We committed ourselves to the Lord and to the people of Perth. They committed themselves to us. We loved each other and we all loved the Lord. There was no stopping us! Soon a new church was being built and Life Bible College was formed. Elmer was supervising the new building programme and teaching in the evenings. I was preaching and doing most of the pastor's work. It seemed nearly everyone who was converted wanted to study and to serve the Lord. The fires of evangelism were spreading in all directions with the message of revival. New churches were starting. It was exciting.

The favourable publicity of the meetings both through the newspapers and the personal witness of so many, brought calls from every side for someone to come and help. Elmer and I hardly had time to speak to each other. Our house was like a dormitory, or more like Grand Central Station. A friend lived with us and many times she cared for the children while I went here and there to answer hospital calls, hold services, counsel people and carry on a radio broadcast. I found my prayer times being interrupted by telephone calls, insistent and demanding. The time I should have been alone with God I would share with someone in need. Hurrying along I'd pray, 'Well, Lord, it looks like I'll have to finish this prayer in the car. I'll just pray as I go.' I kept scooping up my prayers and sermons until one day I hit the bottom of the barrel. I was empty and hollow - and I knew it. I was drained and needed to stop for a refill, but I couldn't stop, it seemed. I was driving on a nearly empty tank and didn't have time to stop at the station. I was surrounded by a host of friends and exciting activity, yet I was feeling inwardly lonelier and emptier.

At the start, when I had tried to leave Perth at that difficult time of decision, Elmer had said, 'No, we're in this together and so we'll either stay here or both go back east together. Compromise is just the devil's trick to get us apart.' So, we had stayed together, but the devil had another trick. He endeavoured to separate us from each other with the work we were doing for God. Elmer was so tired when he came home, working on the church by day and teaching in the school at night, that I didn't have the heart to burden him with my personal needs. Shouldn't I be strong enough for us both during this busy time for him? There was no one else to turn to. My training for the ministry had been full of warnings not to let myself become personally dependent upon any certain member of the congregation, and never to form any personal friendships which could be mistaken for favouritism. 'Familiarity breeds contempt,' I was told. I had a strong strain of self-preservation and independence that made it hard for me to admit that I was in need of anyone else's help. Any way, didn't I have Christ in me? Hadn't I learned that lesson, 'Christ in you, the hope of glory'? Isn't He my sufficiency? I'm complete in Him. Shouldn't I be able to draw on my inner resources and find what I needed by myself rather than crying on my husband's shoulder or admitting my weakness to those to whom I preached? What would they think of me if I, after teaching them that all things were possible, admitted that I was finding it impossible myself to believe and to control my thoughts? My mind felt heavy, sluggish and oppressed. I was finding it hard even to sense the nearness of God.

I was going farther and farther into an emotional wilderness. Where had the wilderness begun? There had been a gradual departure from the green pastures and still waters of personal fellowship with the Shepherd until I felt I was facing my problems alone. The old enemy, self-condemnation, overloaded me with the sense of failure The devil made a 'cat-o-nine tails' and handed it over to me and I thrashed myself endlessly with self-condemnation's whip. 'Aren't you a fine one to be telling others how to overcome! You know what a hypocrite you are!' Preaching, once the joy of my life, became something I dreaded because of the inward scourgings that would follow. My prayers tuned into dirges of unbelief. I could do nothing but tell the Lord how miserably I was failing him and that I realised that I had no right to ask him for anything. Finally, the inevitable lie came. 'Why don't you leave? Wouldn't Elmer be better without you? It's no help to him having you moping around as you are.' True enough, he had been having to plead with me to take my services. Sometimes, because of headaches, I'd convince him that he should preach in my place. Now this happened more and more.

'What about the children?' I'd object. 'I cant' leave the children.'

'They don't need you. They hardly ever see you anyway,' the enemy whispered. 'Others will soon help them to forget you. Go away, Jean.'

'But the church. It would bring such disgrace to the Name of the Lord. It'd be best for me, but what would it do to all those who have trusted me?' my reason would plead.

Back and forth went the argument and I grew weaker, until finally I began to pray the coward's prayer, 'Lord, let me die.'

Everything that I did seemed remote and mechanical. I was acting out of practice, not inspiration. All of this added to my feelings of utter discouragement. Not only by day but by night the tormentor relentlessly took advantage of me. My dreams became full of terror. Another enemy had joined forces with self-condemnation, self-deception. Self-destruction implicitly instructed me in a repetitious night-mare on how to take my life. I would awaken, stiff with fear, unable to even move or call Elmer to help me. I would open my mouth, but nothing came out. I would stare into the darkness waiting for the morning light. Elmer would awaken early, dress quickly, and, giving me a light kiss, would go into the city to work at the church. By the time he came home, I had moved mechanically through another day towards another nightmare.

'You know, Jean,' Elmer said one day, 'I think we should have an evangelist here. We've been slogging away and there is so much work for us both to do. We've been giving out for some time and the people need a change. How about inviting Leo Harris from Adelaide, South Australia, over?'

My heart stirred with hope for the first time in months. 'Yes, I think that'd be good.'

Leo Harris and his wife, Belle, came to minister in our church. They hadn't been there many days when he said quite deliberately at the breakfast table, 'I think the Lord has sent me here to minister in the parsonage more than in the church.' He looked straight at me.

Later, in the hallway outside my bedroom, he stopped me. 'Don't you think maybe we could have a little talk? It might help if we could have some prayer. Aren't you in need of some ministry?' I was cornered. I had tried to avoid this moment ever since he had arrived. At times there had been so much conflict within that I had even sat in our church annexe rather than be directly under the sound of his preaching. Part of me seemed to be saying, 'This is what you need. Ask this man to help you.' The other part screamed within, 'No! No! You can win this battle without his help. Besides, what will he think?'

Leo Harris persisted. "What about it, Jean? Perhaps in the morning you and Elmer could have some prayer with Belle and me. I think the devil is really putting you through it. You're under attack. Maybe I can help.'

I flashed back, pride and self-protection all prickling. 'I am the pastor's wife, you know. I imagine I was preaching the gospel before you knew about it!' I went into my bedroom, closing the door hard behind me. I stood for a moment amazed at my conduct. Then I dropped upon my bed and wept, 'Oh God, help me.' He was, but I wasn't taking it at that point.

It wasn't until the night Elmer found me in the horse paddock behind our house, that all of us realised how much I needed help. I was staring, as if in a trance, at a long black towing rope dangling from the limb of a huge mulberry tree. Johnny and his pals had been swinging on the rope all day. It fitted in perfectly with the nightmare that the devil had brought night after night. 'Go ahead, Jean. Take you life. It's the best way.'

Another time, I was found standing dazed by the river that ran across the bottom of our property. As Leo Harris was leading me back towards the house he asked, 'Why didn't you jump in?' 'Because the devils don't like water,' I said. I was afraid, and I knew for certain that I was under the oppression of the devil. I was ready to let God help me.

How my husband and the Harrises prayed for me! It was an all-out battle against the powers of darkness. Days began to be filled with praise, as in Jesus' name we took back territory that had been lost to the enemy over those dreadful months. I saw my sin and repented.

The accuser had nowhere to stand. Self-condemnation had to flee as I confessed my utter helplessness and cried out for my friends and my husband to pray for me. We opposed the enemy in the battle for my mind. It was war. The Scriptures became the sword of the Spirit, driving back the attack. I repeated over and over verses of promise and affirmation.

'Likewise you that are younger be subject to the elders. Clothe yourselves, all of you, with humility toward one another, for "God opposes the proud, but gives grace to the humble." Humble yourselves therefore under the mighty hand of God, that in due time he may exalt you. Cast all your anxieties on Him, for He cares about you. Be sober, be watchful. Your adversary the devil prowls around like a roaring lion, seeking someone to devour. Resist him, firm in your faith, knowing that the same experience of suffering is required of your brotherhood throughout the world. And after you have suffered a little while, the God of all grace, who has called you to his eternal glory in Christ, will himself restore, establish, and strengthen you' (1 Peter 5: 5-10, RSV).

'No temptation has overtaken you that is not common to man. God is faithful, and he will not let you be tempted beyond your strength, but with the temptation will also provide the way of escape, that you may be able to endure it' (1 Corinthians 10: 13).

'For God did not give us a spirit of timidity but a spirit of power and love and self-control' (2 Timothy 1: 7).

'Fight the good fight of faith; take hold of the eternal life to which you were called when you made the good confession in the presence of many witnesses' (1 Timothy 6: 12). '...having cancelled the bond which stood against us with its legal demands; this he set aside, nailing it to the cross. He disarmed the principalities and powers and made a public example of them, triumphing over them in it' (Colosssians 2: 14-15).

'Thanks be to God, who in Christ, always leads us in triumph' (1 Corinthians 15: 57).

'Finally, be strong in the Lord and in the strength of his might. Put on the whole armour of God, that you may be able to stand against the wiles of the devil. For we are not contending against flesh and blood, but against the principalities, against the powers, against the world rulers of this present darkness, against the spiritual hosts of wickedness n the heavenly places. Therefore take the whole armour of God, that you may be able to withstand in the evil day, and having done all, to stand. Stand therefore, having girded your loins with truth, and having put on the breastplate of righteousness, and having shod your feet with the equipment of the gospel of peace' above all taking the shield of faith, with which you can quench all the flaming darts of the evil one. And take the helmet of salvation, and the sword of the Spirit, which is the word of God. Pray at all times in the Spirit, with all prayer and supplication. To that end keep alert with all perseverance, making supplication for all the saints...' (Ephesians 6: 10-18).

I began to feel the protection of the helmet of salvation as I let my mind be released from the lies and the guilt of the enemy. 'It is written…' was hurled like a hand grenade again and again into the deep trenches within my mind. What the devil said was counteracted by, 'But God's Word says…'

I identified with the account of St Paul's battle with despair and clung to the story that was so much like my own. 'For we do not want you to be ignorant, brethren, of the affliction we experienced in Asia; for we were so utterly, unbearably crushed that we despaired of life itself. Why, we felt that we had received the sentence of death; but that was to make us rely not on ourselves but on God who raises the dead; he delivered us from so deadly a peril, and he will deliver us; on him we have set our hope that he will deliver us again' (2 Corinthians 1:8-10).

Then one evening, the last accusation was confronted. 'She may win this battle, but she'll never have the anointing that she once had. She's lost that. She'll never have power to bring help to others, even though she's been rescued herself. She's lost her anointing.' I felt the cunning suggestion slither through my thoughts that is would be safer for me never to speak about devils or attempt to minister to others as I was being ministered to. It could mean that I would be under attack myself and would probably not be able to overcome! Why not settle for a simple message of salvation, even the baptism of the Holy Spirit and healing, but don't touch this ministry of deliverance.

As I waited trembling before the Lord, His Word came freshly to me, renewing my mind. I recalled with crystal-like clarity how He had spoken the night He had called me into the ministry at the age of fifteen. 'The Spirit of the Lord is upon me, because He has anointed me to preach good news to the poor. He has sent me to proclaim release to the captives and recovering of sight to the blind, to set at liberty those who are oppressed, to proclaim the acceptable year of the Lord' (Luke 4:18). Broken, but yielded, I slowly repeated those words, offering myself to His ministry to the oppressed. I made a deliberate dedication. The devil departed from me and I arose from my knees in the power of the Spirit. I knew that I still had a sacred appointment, and anointing that abode in me permanently, There was still much to learn, but He would teach me. The condition was that I must abide, live, never to depart, rooted to Him, knit to Him, just as His anointing had taught me. (Amplified New Testament 1 John 2: 27).

I had to tell the church what had happened to me, confessing my descent into discouragement and despair, and how Jesus, the Deliverer, had come and brought me out. I told how I had been struggling through a long, long black tunnel mentally. Occasionally I'd seen a faint glimmer of light that had made me move forward, but not without the feeling that I was utterly alone and would probably never make it out. At last, when I had emerged out of the sewer of oppression and torment, I had found that my Saviour had emerged with me. He had never left me! He had gone through it with me! He had been the restraining hand in the darkness that had kept me from running away; from destroying myself. As I told the congregation, my heart melted with thankfulness. It was impossible for me to explain the quality of God's love that had lingered when I had been so unfaithful in my heart, and often with my lips had spoken so harshly to him and to his children. How ashamed I was. At times I had so utterly disbelieved his word. Most of all, I was thankful he hadn't answered my cowardly prayer, 'Lord, let me die!'

Afterwards, I discovered that many of the members in the church had been aware of my struggle. They had watched, prayed and fasted with deep love and understanding, claiming the victory for me. They had suffered with me and they had triumphed with me. How foolish my fears had been as to what they would think. If only I had known!

My husband, too, had been shown by the Lord how needy I was long before I realised he knew. That was the main reason he had invited Rev. Harris and his wife over to the west. How blind I had been, so deceived by the enemy. No one had left me, but I had allowed the enemy to hole me in and isolate me from my dearest ones. I determined never again to mistrust them, or feel too independent or too proud to say, 'I need you. Please help me.'

CHAPTER NINE

RELEASE TO THE CAPTIVES

It seemed that a spiritual hot line went into action immediately. From all directions troubled people began to come to us with every form of demonic oppression. Some were bound mentally, some physically and some emotionally. Mostly, they were tied up in all three ways. They brokenly confessed to deeply embedded hatreds, uncleanesses, phobias and fears. We were swamped with people who were in desperate need and soon our house was full of people who would not, or could not, go home. They were anxious to have the full victory. It was their right. We knew now, by my experience, that no Christian should be constantly oppressed by the devil. Suddenly, we seemed to be thrown in at the deep end of a new ministry. We didn't tread water, that is we didn't ignore the crisis, but we didn't expertly swim, either. We felt out of our depth, but we reached out to help those who were going down, maybe never to rise again. Consequently, there was much excited, over-emotional thrashing around as we tried to deal with devils and men. We were soon tired out. Still we continued ministering in church and parsonage non-stop. One of our Bible college students wisely suggested that if we continued this way, we'd collapse and neither the church nor the college would be helped by that. Elmer and I recognised the devil's same clever trick. If he couldn't keep us out of this ministry, he'd heap it upon us until we broke under it.

To everyone's surprise, Elmer suggested that those who were staying with us should go home. He advised them that he and I were going to take time aside with the Lord and we would let them know what God told us to do. It was obvious that we were not doing this ministry the right way. With some, there had been hours and hours of strenuous ministry extending over several weeks. Something was wrong. 'This is not the way Jesus would do it,' Elmer said.

Several important facts emerged from the confusion and conflict, as Elmer and I took time to quietly wait on the Lord.

First, we had not relied enough upon the Holy Spirits gifts. We had relied too much upon ourselves, and even upon the enemy. There had been occasions when demonic spirits had actually cried out their names. Foolishly we had become involved in the time-consuming practice of asking them when they came in and what they were doing in the person's life. Jesus, in John 8: 44, clearly stated that Satan speaks lies for he is a liar and the father of lies. We had been led into error by the enemy himself. No wonder Jesus forbade devils to speak (Mark 1:34)! We had depended upon our own intelligence to interpret the enemy's words and observed the attitudes of the oppressed, rather than depending upon the wisdom of God through the gifts of the Holy Spirit. We studied the nine spiritual manifestations described by Paul in 1 Corinthians 12:4-11. There is the utterance of wisdom, the utterance of knowledge, the gifts of healing, faith, the working of miracles, the ability to distinguish between spirits, various kinds of tongues and their interpretation, as well as prophecy. The operation of these gifts is totally dependent upon the will and work of the Holy Spirit. All of them are inspired by the Holy Spirit and apportioned, individually as he wills.

Elmer and I realised we had grieved the Holy Spirit by trying to help these people in our own strength. The thing we needed the most was to keep filled with the Holy Spirit. That is why Jesus had sent this abiding Teacher to us. He wanted us to receive his power in order to perform his ministry. Suddenly Acts 10: 38 became so meaningful: 'How God anointed Jesus of Nazareth with the Holy Spirit and with power; how he went about doing good and healing all that were oppressed by the devil, for God was with him.'

Another thing we learned was we had not ministered with the authority that belongs to believers. Jesus won his personal victory over Satan in the wilderness and later exercised that victory during his ministry by the Word of God. We read again and again the passages described in Luke 4: 1-13 and 32-36. Linking these to Luke 10: 17-21 we saw that his authority was delegated to believers. We have authority over all the power of the enemy. We have weakened the effectiveness of that authority by our lack of the use of the Scriptures more often. Jesus cast out the evil spirits by the spoken word, we read in Matthew 8: 16. He always spoke the word with authority and that is why the devils cried out and the people praised God. The words he used were the words the Father gave him, both the written word, as in Luke 4: 12 and words given him to speak (John 14: 24).

Our lack of authoritative ministry based upon the knowledge and use of Scripture had caused us several problems. We had weakened our position by becoming too emotionally involved with those we sought to help. We were operating by strong personal feelings of sympathy for the afflicted and were often too angry with the devil. We had dissipated our energy this way. God showed us that we needed to be operating on a more spiritual level by faith in the Word of God. Here was the place of authoritative, compassionate power.

Also, he revealed to us that some of the people that had come for help really did not want to be delivered, but wanted our time, our attention and our love. He showed us that in order to bring these people to a place of confession of sin and submission to his power, we had to instruct them to depend strongly upon the Word to bring about their deliverance. As we read Hebrews 4:12 we knew that the scriptures were able to do a far better job of sorting them out, than we could. If the person seeking help would accept the word of God, then he was ready to be helped and ready to do his part. If he rejected this sort of ministry, we were to leave him and pray he would be ready later.

In answer to the problem of long sessions of prayer that left both them and us exhausted, God showed us something so obvious that we wondered why we didn't see it before. Jesus would depart into a solitary place to pray before his day's ministry. Or, he would send away those who sought him and go on to a mountain to pray Even when multitudes came for healing, he withdrew himself into the wilderness for prayer. Sometimes he continued in prayer all night. This devotion, this solitary communion, was the secret of his effective powerful ministry. No wonder that by just a word he commanded release to captives. Apparently, prayer was vital to Jesus for this ministry. and must be for us. Personal private prayer is the place of conflict, we suddenly realised. Prayer before we speak to the oppressed. Prayer is not a weapon, but the time we put to use our resources 'in Christ'.

Out of 1 Timothy 2: 1 we heard the call. 'First of all, then, I urge that supplications, prayers, intercessions and thanksgiving be made for all men...' Here is where 'praying in the spirit' (Ephesians 6:18) belongs. It is part of the ministry of intercession. It is resisting the devil; insisting upon full victory for the captives. Here, in the secret place, information and instruction, with gifts of the Spirit, is given to loosen the captives. Here the battle is fought and won before the throne in the presence of the advocate. We contend with the accuser, with the principalities, powers, spiritual hosts of wickedness in high places (Ephesians 6: 12). We stand with the advocate against the accuser, for the accused. With strong, tearful, poured out supplication we quench the fiery darts of the enemy. The passages in James 4: 7 and 1 Peter 5: 6-9 are part of our armoury.

We found the place of power; alone with God, praying in the Spirit. Like the man in the parable of Luke 11, the needy had come to our door. We had found ourselves unable to meet that need. Now we had found the Friend and knew that if we asked he would give. The early Church had done this and we saw the powerful ministry in Acts that followed. 'They continued in one accord in prayer and supplications.' 'When they prayed they were all filled with the Holy Spirit.' They had found the secret of power to minister. That is why Jesus said, 'Tarry until you are endued with power from on high.'

As we waited upon the Lord, He showed us our course of action. We were to invite back to our home for instruction those who were chronically oppressed in some way and had continually sought help, but this time one by one. Instead of dancing to the devil's tune, reacting to the often extreme behaviour of the oppressed, we were to act in the strong authority of those who knew where their power lay.

We were to make appointments according to the time we had to give. When they came, we were to explain that Christians have the right to be free, then we were to select appropriate scriptures and to instruct them to use the verses as a 'scriptural prescription'. They were to repeat them aloud three times a day. We were not to insist that they did a great deal of praying, knowing how the prayers of the oppressed are often dirges of unbelief, but to insist that each morning, noontime and evening they were to read aloud each scripture three times. It was to be audible, directed reading with the mind addressing the Lord Jesus with his Word the first time, addressing his words to themselves the second time, and addressing their foe, the devil, the third time they read. They were to do this for one week and then return for more prayer. In our first prayer and counselling session with them we were to bind the enemy that was oppressing them. In the second session a week later, we were to command every foe to depart from attacking their minds, bodies, and emotions, and for the oppressed person to be released in Jesus' name. The objective was for sin to be confessed. Repentance would bring rejoicing. Of course, this was all with our believing fixed on the efficacy of the blood of Christ and his cross, his resurrection and his position at the Father's right hand.

It worked! They came and we began quietly to counsel and give the powerful prescriptions from the Word of God. Some returned for the second week, others never returned at all. They would not submit to the use of the Word of God. Some would ask to come back earlier than the set appointment, but we refused and urged them to persist with the use of the Word, no matter how distressing it seemed. There were some who were completely delivered before the end of the first week and returned only to praise God with us for the valuable lessons in victory we were all learning.

The Word of God, the person and power of the Holy Spirit, the person of Christ and his blood and his cross, our position with him at the throne, and the armour of God ... all these became supremely significant to us. Minds were renewed, sicknesses, due to evil power, were healed, personalities were released and transformed with a new joyful freedom. No wonder many were filled and refilled with the Holy Ghost. Our students and the oppressed who had been released became a strong team ministering with compassion to others. The life of Jesus flowed through the Body of Christ. We were joined to the Lord, one spirit with him. We were joined in one spirit with the Conqueror.

CHAPTER TEN

RECOVERY OF SIGHT

Several years later we returned to the United States from Australia, Elmer to complete his studies for his degree in Psychology at the California State University in Los Angeles, and I to be an associate pastor at Angelus Temple. Fourteen-year-old Johnny started in high school, and six-year-old LaDonna was an excited beginner in the first grade. Soon after she started in school her teachers informed us that she needed glasses. 'We've moved her to the front seat,' said her teacher, 'and she still can't see the blackboard clearly.'

Concerned, we had her eyes examined by a specialist. He found that she had congenital cataracts. They had been dormant, but now they were active and spreading fast over each eye. 'Nothing can be done, except to prescribe glasses,' the specialist said 'They're too deeply embedded for surgery.' Each visit meant adjustment to her glasses. The lenses were made stronger and stronger as her eyes became weaker and weaker.

We prayed, of course, almost immediately upon receiving the diagnosis. We handed the case over to God. Together, with both of the children, we put our faith in the Lord. This was going to be a family experience. I said to her, 'LaDonna, when you were small we had to claim victory for your healing of eczema. You can't remember that experience. This time you're old enough to understand what we're doing. We're not going to beg God for your healing. We've asked him and now we'll thank him. We'll thank him every time we think of your eyes. We'll thank him for your healing. Okay?'

It was 'Okay', and from that day we didn't act as though we were begging God. We had sought it, claimed it and now we praised him for it. At each time of prayer in our home, every meal and at night before we went to sleep, we praised God for LaDonna's sight. Sometimes a cold fear would steal into my thoughts and I'd find myself wondering how we would cope in a world of darkness. Would I know what to do for a blind child? Promptly I would correct that fear and deny it any room in my mind, 'Lord, I thank you for this trial of faith.' That faith was the brightest thing we had in our lives during those days of waiting.

One day La Donna was sitting beside me in Angelus Temple. We had a guest evangelist, the Rev. Lorne Fox, who has a well known ministry of divine healing. During his message, La Donna whispered to me, 'Mom, I believe today is the day.'

'Hm-m-m? What do you mean? What day?' I asked.

'The day when my eyes will be completely healed.'

I had told her that there would be a day when God would tell her that the waiting time was over and she would receive what we had been waiting for. 'Good,' I said. ' When Rev. Fox finishes his message he'll ask those who are sick to come for prayer. You go up then.' I squeezed her hand and she squeezed mine back, grinning. The glasses wobbled on her nose. We had been waiting for two and a half years!

When Rev. Fox came to pray for LaDonna at the altar, I wanted to stop him. It seemed I ought to explain to him how important this little eight-year-old girl's case was to me. However, I knew that was not going to help faith at all. We prayed. He laid hands on her head and said, 'Receive your healing.'

On the way out of the Temple, LaDonna took off her glasses. 'Well, honey?' I asked. She couldn't see to walk without them.

The time for her next appointment with the specialist came two weeks later. By now the office with its equipment was a familiar place. The doctor sat LaDonna in the same chair and looked into her eyes through the same equipment. He looked up, puzzled. 'Something odd here,' he said. 'Come and look at this, Rev. Darnall,' he motioned to my husband. Elmer peered into the machine and came up beaming.

'You take a look,' he said to me. I no longer saw the dreaded dark spots that we had watched steadily stealing over our daughter's eyes. They were gone!

'What's happened here?' the doctor asked.

'You tell the doctor, LaDonna,' I suggested.

When she had finished, he seemed to have something in his own eyes. He wiped them and said, 'I've heard of things like this happening, but I've never seen it before. Isn't it good of God to do it for one of my patients!' It seemed hard for him to say it, but he knew it, as we did, that she had received a miracle. It was worth waiting!

CHAPTER ELEVEN

THE ACCEPTABLE YEAR

'It'll take a year,' Elmer said when he boarded the plane for Hong Kong. We had just moved into our new home on Huntington Beach, California. John, our son, had enlisted in the United States Air Force and LaDonna was in High School. I planned to do evangelistic work in California until Elmer returned.

I understood why Elmer had to go to Hong Kong. He knew first-hand that there was a job there waiting for someone to do. He had visited Hong Kong when we pastored in Australia. He was shocked that Christian young people had to get their higher education from communist-controlled schools simply because the missionaries had no time to organise a high school. 'We lose so many. They never come back and we don't know what becomes of them. Some of our students would like to continue with us, and to take a Bible course along with their high school studies,but we have no place for them. It breaks our hearts to send them into Communist schools,' the leaders in Hong Kong had told Elmer.

After we returned to the United States from Australia, letters kept coming asking him to organise a high school in Hong Kong. Finally Elmer couldn't avoid the call any longer. God spoke to us when we, at a family altar read 1 Cor 3:11–15. We felt compelled to test our motives for the Christian service we were all doing. He showed us that the 'testing fire' for our works at His Judgement would not be how much we had done, but why we had done it!

The job to be done in Hong Kong would offer no security nor glory but would be more lasting than silver and gold. It was a closed case when the Lord led someone to hand Elmer a cheque for his fare - one way!

Elmer and I kept in close touch by letter tapes. Several weeks after he left, I tucked a potential bomb of a scripture into the middle of my tape. 'You lack one thing' go, sell what you have and give to the poor, and you will have treasure in heaven; and come, follow me.' I didn't want Elmer to know how this text seemed to nag my thoughts and intrude into every quiet moment with an insistence to be noticed. I had tried to make a sermon out of it but it wouldn't jell. The message seemed to be coming toward me rather than out of me! So I wrapped the verse up with news of John in the Air Force and reports of LaDonna's studies. 'By the way,' I said with feigned casualness, 'this scripture has been going over and over in my mind lately. I wonder what it means?' I hurried on, telling other news on the tape, and sent it air mail to Hong Kong.

'Dear Jean,' Elmer's reply tape began. 'You know exactly what that scripture in Mark 10: 21 means. It means what it says. Sell everything you have, give the money away to the poor. God must have something to say but you'll never know what the next step is until you've obeyed.'

Our home in Huntington Beach, the first one we had ever owned was modest, but comfortable, with a swimming pool, and only a mile from one of the best surfing beaches in Southern California. It offered the security we felt we deserved after travelling like gypsies all over the world. It seemed to be in keeping with our years of experience and our position in the church. Yet the word had come to us, 'Sell everything...' and everything it was until the house was empty and I stood leaning against the kitchen door watching the last piece of furniture being carried out. We had carefully selected each piece of early American maple furniture, searching in furniture stores and auctions. I swallowed hard when I saw the maple dining room hutch being carried out. It was one of a kind, and my pride and joy.

'Jean, what are you doing?' I asked myself. Some of my dearest friends thought I was making the mistake of my life! I was selling and giving away everything we had! Some of the things I treasured most were gone, dishes and other articles that had belonged to my mother, paintings and books which meant so much to us were given to other people. The furniture dealers treated my choice pieces that we had paid so much for as though they were junk. What I couldn't sell, I gave away. The 'poor' were young preachers I helped financially. I gave and sold and gave until I judged that, to the best of my knowledge, I had sold and given all.

Standing in the empty kitchen, I asked, 'Now Lord, the next step, the "follow me" part. Where?'

Foxy our miniature Pomeranian dog, jumped around my feet barking. She was excited, running back and forth to the car. This was all that LaDonna and I had left - our dog (we couldn't part with her) and our car, which we felt we had to have if we were going to go any where. In it we packed all the things we needed to live on the road.

LaDonna had helped me through this whole venture. When the Lord had spoken to me about selling everything, I had asked, 'Lord, what about LaDonna? When she was small we took her and her brother with us wherever you called us to go. Now it's different. She's a teenager and can't be taken for granted. She has a personal choice to make here.' I thought of how happy she was with her newly decorated bedroom with its canopied bed. She had a collection of ceramic, glass and wooden carved horses from all parts of the world. They were proudly displayed on shelves around her room. And there were her friends, her school, her church. 'Lord, how can I ask her to leave all that?'

'You won't have to. I'll ask her,' he softly spoke to my heart.

I arrived home late that evening from a service in another town. LaDonna's light was on. 'Honey, you're still up. What's wrong?' I sensed she was upset.

'Mom, I've been praying and the Lord's made it pretty clear to me that you'll have to do lots more travelling. It looks like we'll have to move from here. He's asked me to go with you and...' she hesitated, 'I've just given him my horse collection!'

'Next step, Lord. Where are we to go?' It seemed pretty ridiculous - all packed up and no place to go! I'd tried writing to my friends who had asked me to come to their churches but the typewriter didn't seem to work. My thoughts were jammed. 'Wait a minute, Lord. Don't you want me to write to these pastors?'

'Remember not the former things, nor consider the things of old. Behold, I am doing a new thing; now it springs

110

forth, do you not perceive it? I will make a way in the wilderness and rivers in the desert.'

'Desert, Lord?'

'Yes, I will send you to the desert.'

All I could think of was Death Valley on the Mojave desert!

The yellow telephone on the kitchen wall rang, jarring my thoughts.

'Be quiet, Foxy,; I shouted above her squeals and barking. I grabbed the jangling phone. 'Hello!'

'Hello, is that you, Sister Darnall?'

Closing the patio door to shut out the dog, I replied, 'Yes, but who is this?'

'This is Lee Don Coffee, remember?'

I visualised the blond, blue-eyed, happy-faced young man who had been my talented worship leader in Angelus Temple while he was studying in LIFE Bible College. 'Oh, yes, Lee Don, what a surprise!'

'You promised me that, after I graduated, you'd come and have services for me in my first church, remember?'

'Yes,' I answered cautiously.

'Well, I have a church now and we'd like you to come and hold some services for us. It's just a little church, but since you made the promise, I thought...'

'Lee Don, where is your church?'

'I'm up here in the desert. I'm at Palm Springs!'

It was a little church, seating less than fifty. Quite a contrast to Angelus Temple which seats over five thousand. The attendance was noticeably made up of people from several denominations. The attendance grew until we were compelled to move the crowds to the Pavilion in Palm Springs. Members of many denominations were seeking the power of the Holy Spirit to bring new life to their own churches. They wanted the reality of the New Testament church.

After several weeks of ministry there, LaDonna and I were asking again, 'Next place, Lord!' This was certainly a new way for me to work. Usually there was a well laid out itinerary padded with confirmations and letters of reference and packed with publicity and photographs.

A Lutheran family asked us to Desert Hot Springs next. 'We have a Lutheran Retreat Centre. It will be a nice quiet place for you two to rest. There's no telephone. We would just like you to stay awhile with us and tell us more about the Holy Spirit.'

We moved into a house trailer on the sandy desert, next to the lodge. There wasn't a house in sight, but after Ladonna and I arrived people began to emerge from nowhere like rabbits from under the sage bush. So we had services, with many finding the Lord, and there were some remarkable healings.

A new ministry began, just as the Lord had said, that continued to move us farther and farther from our beloved friends in the Pentecostal denominations towards those in the traditionally non-Pentecostal churches. I became more and more aware of a renewal by the Holy Spirit taking place in denominations that had formerly been very wary and even hostile to the Pentecostal teachings. I discovered that these new or neo-Pentecostals were looking more and more to the classic-Pentecostals, like myself, for teaching. It was not always easy, however, to accept the changes that were taking place. The Holy Spirit's conduct was following much different patterns from those to which I was accustomed. It was hard for me to understand what he was doing and even harder to forecast what he would do next,or how he would do it. I wasn't used to this new way and sometimes I would find myself asking, 'Lord, what are you getting me into?'

This happened once when I was asked by an Episcopalian group to speak to them about the Holy Spirit. I walked into a concktail party! A smiling priest waved his pipe towards me with a friendly greeting.

Where is the group that invited me to speak?" I asked, thinking I was in the wrong place.

'This is the group and we can hardly wait to hear what you have to say about the gifts of the Holy Spirit Jean,' was the reply.

I could hardly wait to get out of there! 'Could you tell me where the ladies' room is, please?'

I was confused. How could these people who seemed to know nothing of the walk in the Spirit, of the deeper life, be filled with the same Holy Spirit that I had received? What of cleansing first, separation to the Lord? To us, smoking and drinking were taboo! I bolted the door. 'Lord, what have you got me into?'

I waited. 'Go in and answer their questions. Forget your sermon notes. Just answer their questions.' I was quite willing to do that. My topic was 'Six Steps Towards A Spirit-Filled Life'. The first step in my notes was, 'Holiness—God never fills an unclean vessel'.

I returned to the packed room. I was as cautious as someone walking on to a frozen lake who wasn't sure how thick the ice was. 'I'll just omit my sermon notes and answer your questions, if you have any.'

'Oh goody, that's just what we hoped you'd do.' A joyous wave of expectancy moved across the room. I felt the warmth of their love. I wasn't on ice, I was walking on the water. I was moving into a miracle.

Their questions were out of an experience that was real and scriptural. They spoke of the Holy Spirit with deep feeling. They knew him. they asked about his gifts and their use in the Church and in their daily lives. They told me of how they had been changed and how their friends were receiving their witness. They were excited, full of wonder and joy. But they shocked me by their unorthodox expressions, such as one young blonde who gushed, 'Oh, having the Holy Spirit inside is like gin in your orange juice!' Later, I asked the Lord about that as I drove along the freeway. 'Did you hear what she said?' I waited and wondered. In a few moments I began to hum a little chorus we sang in Pentecostal churches. Suddenly I remembered the words:

'It's bubbling! It's bubbling! It's bubbling in my soul.
　　There's singing and laughing since Jesus made me whole.
Folks don't understand it, nor can I keep it quiet.
　　It's bubbling, bubbling, bubbling, bubbling, Bubbling day and night.'

I laughed, 'Okay, Lord, that's gin in your orange juice!'

It was not long before I had to face up to the truth that my pride and critical definition of spirituality was a worse stench in the nostrils of God than my new friends' worldly habits. I learned that God does not always work 123456, as I had it down in my notes, but often his way goes 624351! It was hard not to shout' Hallelujah!' when I heard one of that Episcopalian group say that God had made him sick! He explained that, although he had changed his brand of cigarettes three times that week, he still got sick every time he smoked. Before I could say anything, one of his friends said, 'You kook, you, don't you understand? Your body is the temple of the Holy Spirit now, and there isn't any room for that stuff any more.' Another man quickly spoke up, 'Well, my wife and I decided that we would move the bar out of our living room. It didn't seem right to be serving drinks while we talked to our neighbours about the Holy Spirit.' I didn't shout 'Hallelujah! I told you so' because I hadn't told them so, God had! Keeping my mouth shut was the greatest miracle of all.

CHAPTER TWELVE

NO LONGER STRANGERS

LaDonna and I were travelling up the west coast of the United States when the Lord spoke to us that we should go to Europe. 'When, Lord?' October 1st, was the date he gave. From that moment it was called our 'Faith Date'. Each place we went we told of our plan to go to Europe. We had no tickets and we didn't know exactly where in Europe, but we believed that God had a plan. Friends who wanted to share in this adventure with the Holy Spirit asked if I would write a newsletter. They agreed to take the responsibility for mailing it out. 'We're interested in your ministry,' someone wrote in a letter to me. Anxious not to take any glory from the Lord, I replied in my letter, 'It is not my ministry but HiS Ministry.' I saw the typographical error. I started to correct it. Then I saw it was not a mistake. HS had been my abbreviation in my sermon notes to denote the Holy Spirit. It was HiS ministry. The Holy Spirit with a little "i" in the middle. So the Foundation for HiS Ministry was formed by those friends. I accepted this as God's way to help LaDonna and me to minister to the missionaries as we visited, not only Europe but on to the Orient where we would meet Elmer. He had been away for over a year. It would take him two years to get the high school organisation finished. After that, we would return with him to the States.

In Oakland, California, David Du Plessis, a world renowned leader in the charismatic movement, asked me to attend a service where the Rev. Michael Harper, editor of *Renewal* magazine and director of the Fountain Trust movement in Britain, was to speak. The Harpers were delighted when they heard that LaDonna and I were coming to Europe. When we told them our Faith Date, October 1st, they were sure I was to be the speaker for a meeting they had prescheduled in London on that date.' They said, 'It must be you.'

We arrived with forty-four pounds of luggage each, the airline's maximum allowance. The dog had been given away and the car sold. Jeanne Harper met us at the airport and packed us into her mini car along with our luggage. Darting through the peak-hour London traffic on the 'wrong side' of the road, with double-decker buses towering around us, made me feel a little nervous. 'I appreciate that sign. It's a real morale-booster,' I said.

'What sign?' Jeanne asked craning her neck to look up.

'There. That big red sign that says, "Courage. Take Courage".'

She laughed, 'That's a beer advertisement!'

Later that day LaDonna and I were settled in a small room at the Foreign Missions Club in Highbury, a suburb of London. The room was a converted linen closet, made into a bedroom! We were so crowded that one of us had to sit down on the bed to let the other one pass. After I got into bed, I began to giggle.

'What's wrong, Mom?' LaDonna asked sleepily.

'Oh, nothing, except I was just thinking. Isn't it wonderful that the Lord made us get rid of that houseful of things and all the things we stuffed into the car that we thought we just had to have. He knew we'd never get into this room otherwise!'

We both laughed. 'And how would we ever have driven that big Ford Mercury on these narrow streets?'

'Or parked it!' LaDonna added.

After the service in the Metropolitan Tabernacle and in other churches around London, LaDonna and I went on to Paris, then to Berlin, Stuttgart, Hanover and Hamburg. It was winter and ice froze several inches thick on the streets. I received a letter from Michael Harper inviting me to return to England before continuing south to Italy. "No thanks, Michael,' I wrote. 'I nearly froze in October when we were there. I'm not likely to return in January! I never saw a place with so many chimneys and so little fire!' I hardly prayed about it. It didn't occur to me that God had started implementing his plans and dismantling mine.

During the night LaDonna awakened. "Mom, wake up.' She shook me. 'The Lord has told me something. We are going back to England and we'll stay there for a while.'

'Roll over,' I muttered. 'You're having a bad dream.'

In the morning I discovered that my fifteen-year old daughter and the Lord were agreed. We went back to England. Of course, how was I to know that it is warmer in London than it is in Berlin in the winter?

It was not long before I was absolutely convinced that my European itinerary had to be forgotten. All over Britain there were so many who were eager to hear about the renewal and the work of the Holy Spirit in the Church today. Vicars and their wives, curates and parochial church councils, along with congregations, were hungry and ready to

119

receive the Spirit's fullness. Miracles of reconciliation and deliverance transformed lives, ministries and churches.

Then Michael Harper suggested that I go to Poole, in Dorset. He explained that there was a good sized group of people who were keenly interested and met regularly. "The Rev. Ken Prior will meet you,' he said. 'He's the vicar of St Mary's, Poole.'

I got off at the wrong station! I had the vicar's telephone number. He instructed me good naturedly to take the next train and get off at the next station. 'How will I recognise you?' I asked.

'Watch for the dog collar.' It was a sign that I had looked for more than once!

The Rev. Ken Prior was a tall, cheerful man who was anxious to tell me how things were progressing in the area. 'There are a number of lay people and several clergy who have been filled with the Spirit. Another pastor and myself have led the group along. I'm afraid we have a full schedule for you. We've arranged several speaking engagements for you, and a number of people want to meet you for counselling.'

It was a busy schedule, so when I noticed I had a luncheon appointment, I asked him if he thought I really needed to go. He thought it would be best for me to lunch at Post Green. 'Faith Lees will pick you up tomorrow at noon,' the vicar said.

I got up extra early the following morning to allow time for prayer. 'Lord, I'm willing to remain, at least until Elmer comes and joins us here. For LaDonna's sake, may I please find a place for us to unpack and where she can be settled. We have no home here. We're strangers. We need a place to roost somewhere.'

Suddenly the vision appeared within my mind. It had come twice before. I saw the British Isles glistening like a clump of jade in the grey seas surrounding them. It was a bird's eye view. Looking down I saw Scotland, England, Wales and to the northwest, Ireland. The tree tops upon the hills and the clustered clouds hid the people. Suddenly small, flickering lights appeared. they were scattered all over the isles. I came closer to the land. The light was firelight. There were fires burning from the top of Scotland to Land's End on the tip of Cornwall. Lightning streaked downward from the sky above me. I saw it touch down with flashing swiftness, exploding each of the fires into streams of light. Like lava, they burned their fiery path downward from the top of Scotland to Land's End. The waters did not stop them, but the fire spread across the seas to Ireland and to Europe!

'Lord, this is the third time you've shown me this vision during prayer. Could you give me the meaning of it?' I asked, deeply moved by the Holy Spirit. He revealed to me that the small fires all over the land were groups of earnest, hungry people who were being drawn together by the Holy Spirit to study their Bibles and to pray for a visitation of the Holy Spirit. the words 'pockets of power' were impressed upon my mind. 'I'm empowering them by my spirit and I'm teaching them by my spirit about my gifts. They are being led by my spirit to repentance, reconciliation and a deeper relationship with the Body of Christ. These people are meeting in homes and churches. I'm not leading them out of their relationships in the home and the church, but into a deeper involvement in both. They are to bring renewal, new life, in preparation for what is to come.'

'What is to come, Lord?' I asked, wondering why he should show this to me.

'I will penetrate the darkness with a visitation of my power. With lightning swiftness I will release the power of my spirit through a renewed people who have learned how to be led of the Spirit. They will explode with a witness that will touch every part of the society of Britain. I am strategically placing them to touch the farms, villages, towns and cities. No one will be without a witness whether they be children in the schools, farmers in the fields, workers in the factories and docks, students in the universities and colleges, the media, the press, the arts or government. All will be profoundly moved and those who are changed by my power will alter the destiny of the nation'

'And the streams of fiery light into Europe, Lord?' My mind seemed to see an army of all types of people moving into the continent with a compassionate ministry. This ministry was not mass meetings, led by powerful personalities, preaching to spectators, but participating, caring communities involved with each other at a grass roots level, sharing the love of God everywhere. I saw the empty cradles of Europe, her churches, holding a new generation of Christian leaders.

'Are you ready?' called the vicar. My new friend, Faith Lees, was waiting at the bottom of the stairs. She was slim, dressed in faded blue jeans, shirt-tail out. Her fresh complexion, blue eyes, short, windblown hair and wide friendly grin, made her look remarkably young. Driving along that afternoon, I suddenly realised that she must live in the country. The lovely town of Poole was behind us. We were travelling into some pleasant countryside with green fields and thatched roofed cottages. I found myself longing to see inside one of those cottages and hoped my driver lived in one. Faith was telling me how she and her husband, Tom, were filled with the Spirit and were conducting Bible studies. Suddenly we swung into a driveway and pulled up in front of a Georgian country home. 'Well, here's Post Green!' she said as she hopped out of the car. I followed her to the door and stepped in. A big, brown shaggy sheep dog loped in behind me. Faith glanced towards him. 'That's Bear.' I had stepped into a wide reception hall. A spiral staircase led up two storys. My eyes followed its graceful railing. Above me hung a giant crystal chandelier. We turned to look out of the French doors that faced the garden. Park-like grounds stretched out before us and huge beech trees that looked as though they had stood there forever shaded the ground near the house. Flower beds bordered the lawns. 'Isn't this beautiful!' I whispered, awed by the immensity of it all.

'Why are you whispering?' Faith asked me as she leaned, relaxed, against the glass door.

'Well, where is the lady of the house?' I asked, expecting to see someone appear any minute.

Faith stood up straight. 'I'm the lady of the house,' she said, smiling.

I suddenly wished I hadn't come, for she was a 'real' lady, a titled English lady, Lady Faith, and her husband, she told me, was Sir Tom Lees. 'This is Tom's family estate, but since we've come close to the Lord, we realise that it really all belongs to him and we're his stewards.'

During lunch they told me that the Lord had caused them to feel that I was in need of a place where LaDonna and I could stay and where we could get some rest. I really hadn't had anything like this in mind when I had asked our Heavenly Father that morning for a place to roost!

'We want you to know that you're both welcome,' Sir Tom was saying. 'We have a room up in the wing that we thought would give you a bit of privacy and quiet.' It would have been easy to say, 'Tell me when to move in,' but I knew that this was going to be a choice that would completely alter our purposed path.

'Thank you,' I replied. 'I want you to know that your kind offer is more than I could ever have dreamed possible to happen to me. It would be easy to say "Yes" immediately, but I must have a little time to pray about it and also to talk to LaDonna.'

'Of course,' they both agreed.

My next meeting was near London at Thames Ditton. I never mentioned the prospects of remaining in England in my service, nor anything about the Lees' kind offer. I must confess that, when I put my head on the pillow that night and closed my eyes, I visualised the wide, spacious lawns of Post Green. Also in the morning the memory was there again.

'Lord,' I prayed as I opened my Bible, 'You know how I ask you for three witnesses when I have an important decision to make. I have the first one, the feeling in my heart. But one witness is not dependable. Please give me the other two witnesses that will perfectly agree with the first one. I need the scriptural witness and the independent one - a circumstance of personal direction through someone else that will agree with the other two. I picked up my Amplified New Testament to read my selected daily reading. I knew that a scriptural witness found by going through the Bible selecting what I wanted, or by going through the promise box, wouldn't be satisfactory. It had to come quite easily without searching. It had to be given to me. I began the Bible reading that I had planned for my morning prayer time. It was 1 Corinthians 16. I had read a couple of verses when the lady with whom I was staying knocked at the door. 'Sorry to disturb you Jean,' she said, 'but a letter's arrived for you.'

'Thanks, Dorothy.' I took the letter. It was from Post Green. 'Just want to put in writing our invitation so that you'll know we really mean it.' I laid the letter down and sighed. 'Lord, it would be so easy to go, but I must wait until you give me complete confirmation.' I picked up my New Testament. The next verse said, 'But it may be that I will stay with you (for a while), perhaps even stay the winter. so that you may bring me forward on my journey to wherever I may go!'

I laughed, 'All right, Lord, that's as if you wrote it to me today! Witess number three please.'

Dorothy put her head in the doorway again. 'There's a lady on the phone and she'd like to see you before you leave today.'

I don't know if I can. There's a vicar coming this morning who wants to receive the power of the Holy Spirit.' I paused. 'Oh, tell her that I can give her ten minutes if she can come right away, would you, Dorothy?'

When I met her in the lounge, she seemed a little shy. 'Can I help you?' I asked. I thought there must be some urgent need that required prayer. She hesitated. I looked at her closely. 'I don't have much time. Could you just let me know what I can do for you?'

'Well, it's not for me to try and tell you what the Lord's will is…' she began to apologise. 'I've never done anything like this before.' I suddenly sensed the familiar awareness one has when about to hear a word from the Lord.

'My dear, do you have something to tell me? Has the Lord sent you with a message?'

'Yes, I suppose you could say that,' she faltered.

'Come on,' I encouraged her, getting excited. 'Come on, I'm waiting. Tell me.'

'Well, in prayer this morning I felt strongly impressed to tell you that you and your daughter must not leave England but stay here for as long as the Lord has need of you.'

'Oh, thank you!' I said. 'You don't know it, but you're my third witness.'

She looked surprised, but pleased and relieved.

'You know, I've never done anything like this before. Anglicans just don't do this sort of thing!'

I sent a postcard to Faith with just the reference, 1 Cor. 16: 6, printed in the middle, and signed it.

Her card was waiting at the next place, 'Dear Jean, 2 Tim. 4: 21, Faith.' I hurriedly opened my New Testament. The verse read, 'Do hasten and try your best to come before winter'!

By the time Elmer came from Hong Kong, the winter had passed, spring, that season that turns all of England into a lovely garden, had come and gone, and summer was almost over. In those fleeting months LaDonna and I had seen the hand of God produce an astonishingly fast growing fellowship at Post Green. Ministers in the area asked Sir Thomas if we could have conferences at his house. The drawing room filled up, then the dining room overflowed and people sat on the staircase listening, leaning over the railing from the floor above. After the conferences, came camps, which drew young people from all parts of England. We had just finished our youth camp when Elmer arrived.

Welcome Home!

So then you are no longer strangers and sojourners, but you are fellow citizens with the saints and members of the household of God. Eph. 2:19.

The brightly painted words were stretched out on a piece of butcher wrapping paper across the bedroom wall. 'They really mean it, Elmer,' I said as we stood in the middle of the master bedroom at Post Green. Elmer was staring at the hastily written sign. 'Sir Thomas Lees and Lady Faith - everyone here at Post Green is so loving and genuine.' I squeezed his hand. 'As you get to know them you'll under-stand,' I said, glancing back at the text on the wall.

Elmer was tired. he had arrived that afternoon on the air flight from Moscow to London. He had travelled across Russia on a long, slow train journey from Siberia. Before that he had sailed from Hong Kong to Vladivostok. It was no wonder he was finding it hard to take in the meaning of the warm welcome to a place he had never seen, extended to him by British people whom he had never met! Elmer sat down wearily near the window of the bedroom, and looked out over the restful green lawns and gardens. His eye lingered to study the Norman tower of the village church that stood in the field beyond. It was a clear day. We could see the blue Purbeck Hills beyond the harbour. As I glanced at Elmer, I realised he wasn't seeing it at all. He was still in the crowded Kowloon tenement district of Hong Kong. He could still hear the sing-song voices that chirped day and night along with the clatter of the crowded streets that are never empty. He couldn't see what I saw in England. It was too soon. But neither of us could see what lay ahead - a ministry from Post Green that would bless the nation. A gong sounded. It seemed far away, oriental. We were startled. 'Dinner's ready,' Tom called out.

In time, Elmer began to think of England as home and the sounds of Hong Kong seemed far away.

The following spring two young people, Valerie Lester and Tony Churchill, came to Elmer. 'Why don't you start a Bible college here?' they asked. After prayer he said, 'If we have six students we'll start.'

Six months later, Christian Life College started with twelve students. It offered a full curriculum in Biblical studies, plus practical instruction for Christian service. The evening classes allowed students time to work during the day and to live where they pleased. This was unique for England, where Bible Colleges and seminaries are residential and mostly denominationally oriented. Students from traditional churches that were renewed by the Holy Spirit came. Teachers from Anglican, Baptist, Congregtional, Brethren and Pentecostal backgrounds who had been filled with the Holy Spirit came. Drawn together by the Holy Spirit from Britain and other countries, more than a hundred were attending the classes.

From Post Green a loving ministry that began with Sir Thomas Lees and Lady Faith expanded through a team of dedicated workers who lived in the neighbourhood. Family camps, youth camps and conferences, along with ministerial symposiums, allowed full scope for experience in the ministry of the Holy Spirit. To those who could not attend our college or did not live nearby, Post Green sent a Correspondence Leadership Training Course.

We were feeding the fires God lighted. His fires would become pockets of power; power built up for a spiritual explosion to shake the nation. Witnesses would flow, like rivers of fire, over the land from the north to the south.

Streams of people with apostolic power would witness on the streets, everywhere.

I began to perceive God had more to say about the rivers of fire that would flow across the English Channel and over Europe. The word 'communicators' kept coming to mind as I prayed. Communicators? That was a new word for ministry. God calls missionaries, evangelists. Does he call communicators?

"I will call and equip skillful, creative communicators to witness for me in Europe," I sensed him say. Then I could see them: musicians, artists, vocalists, technicians, journalists, actors . . . all Spirit-filled and prophetic. It was then I knew that the wave of spiritual awakening that will hit Europe will impact the masses through the media. First, the media, then it will flow into the churches. In Britain it would flow from the churches, into the streets, then through the media. In Europe, Christian communicators will impact the general public through the media, and then the impact will hit the churches. I could see the dark cathedrals of Europe light up.

CHAPTER THIRTEEN

LET THERE BE LIGHT

A man called Peter Hill phoned,' Elmer said. 'I'd just returned from another long journey. More and more my ministry took me away from home to different parts of Britain. I went anywhere the Lord sent me, from the stately Birmingham Cathedral to a tiny Belfast house in the riot area. Exhausted, but deeply satisfied, I would return home to Rest Harrow, the house God had loaned us in the quiet countryside near Post Green.

It was hard for me to focus on Elmer's telephone message. 'Peter Hill? I don't believe I know him.'

'You don't know him,' Elmer said. 'He called from London and has invited us to a committee meeting of some kind.'

'A committee for what' I asked. I rather distrusted committees.

'He said he had heard about your vision for a spiritual awakening in Britain. There are a number of other people who share the same impression that something is going to happen in Britain - or at least needs to. Peter Hill feels that everyone with such a vision should get together, and so he's called this meeting,' Elmer explained.

'It may be what we've been waiting for,' I said. We both had a growing impression there needed to be a positive demonstration of Christian witness in London. We envisaged young people coming from all parts of Britain to a mass rally for Christ.

It was what we were waiting for! God had brought together an assorted group of Christians from different parts of the Church. They were united by a single vision.

The chairman of the group that met was Col. Orde Dobbie, retired from military service but fighting for the needs of the underprivileged as general secretary of a social service organisation. Others of the group that would later form an executive committee included a professional actor, concerned to relate Christianity to the arts, and an Anglican rector, formerly a shop steward and a trades unionist, who wrote for the Church of England Newspaper. He had taken a strong stand against pornography and had led protests against obscene and blasphemous plays in London theatres. The general secretary of the Evangelical Alliance joined us as well. These, with several others who later came to help, drew out plans to fulfill the vision.

A twin purpose was envisaged: to protest against the exploitation of sexual behaviour in the media and the arts, and to proclaim the Christian gospel as the positive answer to the problem.

It was obvious that two rallies would be necessary, one to represent a civic protest against moral pollution, while the other would proclaim the gospel and present the claims of Christ. The two meetings would be linked by a March of

Witness. We had six months to bring thousands together to London! "Can it be done?' we wondered. 'It must be done,' we decided. 'It shall be done,' God's word promised!

It was done, not by might, nor by power but truly by His Spirit. God sent help from all kinds of people, the unknown and the well known. Malcolm Muggeridge, British journalist and philosopher, gave his full support even to the extent of christening the whole event the Festival of Light.

My vision of fires burning all over Britain was quite literally fulfilled as Operation Beacon Light, suggested by an Anglican vicar who knew nothing of our vision, was enacted. Beacon fires were ignited on strategic hilltops throughout Britain to alert the nation to the dangers threatening moral health and family life itself. Thousands of people marched and congregated near the beacon fires to hear civic and church leaders speak out against the moral landslide and to call for a public demonstration offering a positive solution to the problem.

On the day of the festival, Trafalgar Square was packed with over 35,000, and the vision, like a still shot in a movie, suddenly came to life. The speakers were a combined cross-section of society: Lord Beswick, Chief Labour Whip in the House of Lords, and Mrs Peggy Fenner, a Conservative MP; the managing director of a paper company and a left-wing shop steward; a young Salvation Army officer and a Roman Catholic house wife; David Kossoff, the Jewish actor, and Nick Cuthbert, one of our own students from Christian Life College; and Malcolm Muggeridge and Mary Whitehouse, a notable promoter of Christian values in television. They spoke to an enthusiastic crowd. Proclamations were read out in the square to the government, the media and the Church. Thousands of young voices punctuated the speeches with shouts of 'Jesus... J - E - S - U - S...JESUS!'

Then the March of Witness streamed out from Trafalgar Square toward Hyde Park, singing, shouting the name of Jesus and inviting everyone along to join them for the rally. Stranded motorists and tourists who couldn't get through the crowds watched in curious wonder at this unlikely demonstration of love and concern.

The Trafalgar Square rally was a citizens' demo that gave an opportunity for everyone who was concerned about the nation's moral pollution problems to express themselves. MORAL POLLUTION NEEDS A SOLUTION read the bold banner displayed across the platform there.

The Hyde Park Rally was a Christian demonstration. Our banner read, "Jesus Is The Solution!" Our team of speakers included the Rev. Tony Sergent of Worthing Tabernacle and of the Westminster Fellowship; the Rev. David Watson, a young Anglican clergyman from St Cuthbert's, York; the Rev. David MacInnes, precentor of Birmingham Cathedral; and myself. I represented the Pentecostal tradition. There were gospel groups from Britain and the United States singing. The young actor, Nigel Goodwin, called on young people to give testimonies. Cliff Richard added his super testimony in word and song. Arthur Blessitt of the Jesus Movement in America, who was carrying his cross through Britain, laid it down to join us for that day.

As the sun was setting, a multitude numbering over 100,000, according to the press reports, knelt in Hyde Park to pray for the nation. Even English policemen were kneeling, hushed before the presence of God. Suddenly someone began to sing the Lord's prayer. At that moment we all felt what one writer later described: 'The Festival of Light was a timely and necessary manifestation of the presence of God.'

It did not end on that day. It continued through the year with regional rallies and marches across the country. Action groups formed to enforce Operation Newsagent in an attempt to arouse the conscience of newsagents and their customers regarding the hard core pornography that lay next to children' comics and family magazines. Thousands of signatures were gathered to back up a petition for decency that was presented to the Prime Minister. Debates took place in schools, universities and Parliament. There was dialogue between festival representatives and politicians, members of the media and church leaders. Intercessors for Britain, a prayer movement, continued to grow as more Christians became concerned about the needs of the country.

Young people began to learn the meaning of the 'light and salt' concept in Jesus' teaching of discipleship. A manual was produced offering balanced teaching to the young on Loving Jesus Style.

The ground swell continued to increase until another wave of public demonstration broke forth and rolled in over London for an unforgettable five days in the next year. The Jesus Festivals were not only in Trafalgar Square and Hyde Park but in other London parks as well. Teaching centres were held in churches during the day to teach the many young people who had come to Christ throughout the country more about what the Bible has to say regarding marriage, sex, government, church, family relationships and ethics. We were training them for the time when God's lightning-swift Spirit will send a spiritual awakening that will flow like liquid fire from the top of Scotland to Land's End.

In the closing moments of the Hyde Park rally, as Cliff Richard brought the crowd to their feet with his final number, 'How Great Thou Art!', Nigel Goodwin and Gordon Scott, two of the organisers, came up to me. 'Jean, Cliff is just finishing. You've got five minutes. Do you have something to give them?'

'Yes,' The Lord had just spoken to me. As I stood before that crowd of 100,000. I sensed their hunger. I told them how Jesus had stood before a multitude like this one day. He took a child's small offering and blessed it and everyone was fed. That day long ago he gave something miraculous to his followers and told them to feed the multitude. They had bread for every hand that reached out.

'I've got a small amount of time,' I said. I'm turning it over to Jesus and as I pray, I believe he will give you a share of his miraculous power. You who are empty; you who are sick, nauseated within your inner self; you who ache with longing of unfulfilled hopes and dreams; you who desire something wholesome - you've never tasted it, but you know it's there somewhere. You're hungry. Jesus is your bread of life. He'll satisfy your deepest longings for love, pure love, that won't destroy you. Some of you are sick in your bodies and burned out from sin and lust. Your brain bursts with painful memories. Jesus can heal you. He can give you a miracle right now. I can't reach you or touch you, but he can, through his children. I want each of you, his followers, to stretch forth your hands to those around you. Give them your love, you prayers. While I pray, you pray for one another. Give to each other. Pray for one another that you may be healed. It's just a small offering, but the Master will touch it with his miraculous power.'

Thousands of Christians who had been reaching upwards with the Jesus 'one way' sign, reached outwards with open hands, touching others. They linked arms in chains of hundreds. They prayed, confessed, and wept together. A murmur of joyous praise increased, like the sound of flowing water. Hearts opened to Christ, receiving his power.

I prayed, 'I thank you for filling the hungry. I thank you for miracles. Jesus, I thank you that you are the same yesterday, today and forever. Amen.'

CHAPTER FOURTEEN

WHEN YOU COME TOGETHER

The airmail letter on my desk disappointed me. I had not expected it. the peace I had about my trip to United States was shattered. The letter canceled one of the most important speaking engagements I had planned in California. It was two days before I was to leave England. There had been a misunderstanding, it stated. The pastor had returned from a trip abroad and he chose to speak himself on Palm Sunday.

'Palm Sunday.' I was annoyed. 'Of all Sundays. Every pastor I know will have that Sunday booked by now.'

Beverlee, my secretary, sat beside me, pencil and pad ready for dictation. Patiently, she listened as I thought aloud.

'Maybe I shouldn't go. There's plenty to do here.'

We both smiled, looking at the correspondence piled on the desk; much of it invitations from all over Britain.

'Why should I traipse to United States? They don't need me.'

I turned from my desk and gazed out of the study window. The garden was awakening to spring. Yellow daffodils swayed in the gentle breeze, seagulls flew over the sloping green hills towards Poole Harbor. 'It's so beautiful here. Why should I go anywhere?' I murmured.

Turning towards the desk, I took the letter, looked up and asked, 'Lord, what do you want me to do about Palm Sunday?'

'Write to Jack Hayford in Van Nuys,' I heard myself saying aloud.

'Jack Hayford?' Beverlee echoed.

'Yes. He's a pastor I know. This is contrary to the way I usually work, but I feel it's right. In fact, I would say God wants me to do it. Take a letter to Jack Hayford, The Church On The Way, Van Nuys, California. I will let him know I am available Palm Sunday. God must have a reason for changing these plans.

It was only eight o'clock in the morning when I drove up in front of The Church On The Way on Palm Sunday. The wide boulevard was nearly empty of traffic. There was a Sunday morning sleeping-in stillness over the neighborhood. Yet in front of the plain, small, green, stucco chapel a crowd stood on the steps, overflowing on to the sidewalk.

Jack Hayford had advised me to come early. 'You need to see what is happening in our church before you speak in the evening, Jean. I would like you to come at eight in the morning.'

'For Sunday School?' I asked, rather mystified.

'No, for service. You see, we have multiple services now to accommodate the crowds.'

By the time I parked the car and got around to the front of the church, the doors were open and the church was filling fast. Jack Hayford was already at the front.

Jack was an associate of ours when we were at Angeles temple. I well remembered the strong, confident, active extrovert who was so full of optimism and drive. Jack was always able to inspire and stimulate everyone to be as enthusiastic as himself.

As I watched him minister that Palm Sunday morning, I saw a different man. He was still a good talker, but his dynamic personality seemed more dependent upon something other than himself. His manner was mellow and humble. His obvious deep love and respect for his congregation allowed them to speak and share in the service.

Reluctantly, I left early to drive to the Lutheran church where I was to speak for their 11 am service. I pushed my way through the crowd outside who had already gathered for the second service that morning.

"I've got to find out what is happening here,' I thought. I could hardly wait to get back for Jack's evening services, not only to speak, but to listen and to learn.

After the second packed-out service that night, I met with Jack Hayford for a chat. In that small church, seating less than three hundred, fifteen hundred to two thousand people had come through to doors in one day! Not only had they attended, but many had participated in a new depth of fellowship with God and with one another. Something had drawn people of all ages and all backgrounds to a sharing, caring situation that made them like one loving family. It was difficult for me, at times, to recognize the distinction between pastor and people. The recognizable structure of pulpit-pew order was dismantled during the services. The people reached upward to God in worship, hands raised, faces aglow. They also, stretched to reach across seats, even got up and walked around and clustered into loving groups for quiet but fervent prayer.

Jack was swallowed up in the movement of the whole church ministering to one another. His submission, willing to be submerged in this way was what interested me most. He seemed able to submerge and to emerge at the right times. How did he do it? What had happened to him and to his church?

"Jack, what has happened here? I know this church has had a rough history of internal trouble and external indifference for years."

Jack, tall, with penetrating brown eyes and strong, serious expression, leaned back and rubbed his hand over his high forehead. 'Jean,' he spoke in his rather sonorous voice, 'I came here, as you know, with the hope of seeing this church resurrected. As you see, something happened, but not in the way I expected. I can take no glory for it.'

He went on, 'While I prayed one day, soon after I came here, I found myself going back over my life in my mind. It seemed God wanted to show me how I have been a leader ever since I can remember. Even in nursery school, I organized things; delegating jobs to the other kids! I was that way all through my adolescent years. Then at college and on into my ministry. I asked God, 'Why are you showing me this, God?'

'You're quite a leader, aren't you, Jack?'

'Yes, God, you made me that way.' I wasn't sure what God was saying.

'Jack, will you turn your leadership position over to me? I've called you to lead my people, but you've placed yourself too far ahead of them. Will you walk as a shepherd with the sheep, for my sake?'

'Jean,' Jack looked straight at me, 'I know God ordains strong leadership but I weakened it by letting by position become too important to me. It had separated me from the very people I wanted to help! God was asking me to turn my position over to him. Believe me, it took some time, but I finally said yes!' At that moment I was ready to accept that I would probably never pastor more than a hundred people. I yielded, and felt peace.

Jack took a deep breath. 'It was after that something wonderful happened. I was alone in the church before the service started. As I walked across the foyer to adjust the thermostat for the heat, I looked into the sanctuary and I saw the glory of God!'

'You could see it? You could see the glory of God?' I asked.

'Yes, it was a golden cloud, like a mist, filling the place. I blinked,' Jack continued, 'not sure I was seeing it right. I am not given to visions, as you know,' he said with a grin. 'God assured me I was seeing it right.'

'It is my glory, Jack, I am placing my name here. I will draw people from far and near. If you will obey me, stepping forth when I say and back when I say, letting me lead, then I will teach you and my people how to minister to me, to each other and to the world.'

Among the thousands God attracted to The Church On The Way was the Owens family. Jimmy Owens, a gifted, sensitive, soft-spoken musician had dedicated himself and his talent to the Lord as a young man. He and his wife, Carol, and two children, Jamie and Buddy, composed, recorded and performed music that blessed people in many parts of the world.

A few days after my talk with Jack Hayford, I met the Owens. It was through Lorna De McPherson, whose husband, Rolf, pastored Angeles Temple. She was really keen to hear all about what God was doing in Britain. During a dinner party I told her about Post Green and the Festival of Light.

Suddenly she asked, 'Have you heard about 'Come Together?'

'Come Together?' I repeated. 'No'

'Well, you ought to take time to meet Jimmy Owens. Carol, his wife, is my cousin. They are composers, Jean. I am sure you should meet them.'

She looked inspired. 'They could be a big help to your festivals and all that is going on in Britain.'

She told me about their music with enthusiasm. As I listened I began to fidget in my mind. My thoughts were moving on to the TV program where I had to appear that evening...It was getting late.

'Sorry, Lorna De. I'm sure I won't have time to meet the Owens on this trip. I fly out in a couple of days to Florida. Besides, we have a lot of talented people in England.' I saw Lorna De's disappointment.

The dinner party began to break up and my friends decided to go with me to KHOF TV Studio to watch the program. Afterwards, Lorna De came up to me. 'Jean, I still feel you ought to meet Jimmy and Carol. Couldn't we arrange something?'

'I'm sorry, Lorna De, I don't see how I can. If you could just see my diary...' I broke off as friends on the other side of the studio called out, 'We will wait for you ever here, Jean.'

Lorna De started to go, them asked, 'Do you have a phone number where I can call you?'

'Yes,' I gave her the number where I stayed in North Hollywood. She gave me a quick hug and smiled. 'I will phone in the morning.'

The next day, in spite of a busy line, Lorna De persevered and finally got me on the phone. 'Jean, I have contacted the Owens. Do you have time to see them tomorrow?'

I had my diary open. 'How about eight o'clock in the morning?' I didn't think she would say 'yes,' but she did.

'Fine at my house.'

Before I could think of any reason not to go, she hung up!

I wasn't my best in the morning. I felt irritable as I drove towards Lorna De's home. My intention was to make this a courtesy call, meet the Owens and hurry on to make plans for my flight to Florida. I slammed the door of the car, and hurried towards the entrance of the garden. Lorna De, beamed with pleasure as she greeted me. It was evident she enjoyed her part in arranging for the Owens and me to meet. She led me through toe courtyard, past the tree ferns and tropical plants towards the front door. Suddenly my disgruntled disposition was checked. Alerted, by the Holy Spirit, I slowed down.

'Listen to this man. I have arranged this meeting.' I knew I was on a mission for the Lord.

Jean, this is Carol and Jimmy Owens.' Jimmy stood tall in the sunny living room. He extended his hand. Carol came in from the dining room. Jimmy, around fortyish, was relaxed and casual. Carol, slim, blue-gray eyes sparkling with curiosity, moved quickly towards me. She said simply, 'Hi,' as if she met me every morning in that same place.

While Lorna De and Carol put the finishing touches to the breakfast, Jimmy and I talked.

I began. 'Jimmy, don't tell me about your music now. Just to me about yourself. What has the Lord done for you?'

Before Lorna De called us to breakfast, Jimmy had told me about The Church On The Way and how God led them there. He told how God had spoken to them in the midst of a productive music ministry, to not write any more music until he gave them the word. The family obeyed, waiting for eighteen months, with considerable sacrifice. One day pastor Hayford casually remarked, as they ate dinner together, 'Jimmy, you haven't written any new music lately. Why don't you write something about the things God is teaching us at the church? Tell how we have come together in ministry to the Lord, to one another, and to the world.

Jimmy said softly, 'I knew the next morning that God had spoken to us through our pastor. The music which had been waiting, began to flow. Carol and I promptly began to write Come Together.

After breakfast they talked of how their music was written to help people to worship the Lord. Also, to teach how to reach out in fellowship with others and how to offer themselves to serve Christ in the world.

I grew excited. 'Why, that is what God is teaching us in Britain. A new sound of fresh, spontaneous, joyous worship is heard wherever people come together. The Holy Spirit helps us to openly share our feelings and our needs with one another and to pray for one another. The Festival of Light proved there are thousands of youth who are ready to respond to the challenge to be salt and light in a corrupt society.' Something touched us as we talked together. We were thrilled, for we began to sense God's purpose.

'Jimmy,' I said, 'I believe Come Together is the next step in preparing Britain for a spiritual awakening.' I was a little startled at my own words. I had not even heard the music. But God had told me to listen to the man, not to his music. Jimmy had the right message for the people of Britain.

As we discussed it, plans were formed for a ten day concert tour. Lorna De beamed with satisfaction as we all agreed in prayer.

'You were right,' I said as I left. 'I was meant to meet Jimmy and Carol. Thanks for being so persistent.'

When I returned to London, I found there were plenty of reasons not to produce the Come Together musical. For one thing, there was no one willing to organize the tour. I approached groups who were well able to promote such an enterprise, but they refused. I showed them a film of a Come Together performance, made in the United States. Those who saw it agreed it had the message Britain needed, but they did not feel it was the right time for it. Others said it was too 'American' and if it was done, it should be done by the British. Also, there was absolutely no money to finance such a huge undertaking.

After a brave attempt to stir up interest in London, I returned to Rest Harrow, disappointed. Elmer and La Donna prayed with me.

'I guess I will have to ask the Lord to help me produce this musical and to show me where he wants it performed. It will take all my time.'

'It looks like you have a new ministry cut out for you,' Elmer said.

Over the next few weeks, I drove hundreds of miles to contact people in Edinburgh, Liverpool, Belfast, Birmingham, Coventry and in London. In each city I found the people God had prepared for the ministry of Come Together. I found a coordinator and a music director in each place. It took trust, based on faith in God, for most of these people I had never met. Usually, I had only one evening to show the film and to share the vision. We selected a date out of the eight days allowed for the concert tour. After I left town, the local coordinator and director had the task of selecting the hall, informing the public and organizing a mass choir!

By the time the preliminary organization was done, God had provided the fares for Jimmy Owens and his family to fly to England. A home was offered for them to use during their stay. Mass choirs were assembled within weeks in every city I had designated. Jimmy started his rehearsal tour. The finances for each concert seemed to take care of themselves. As we went forward by faith, the threat of no money just moved aside. No necessary plan was hindered. Capable, gifted people began to volunteer for every job needed to be done. Publicity spread through magazines, papers and prayer letters, as Christians caught the vision of Come Together.

Pat Boone, gave up his family vacation time, to be our lead singer. When he arrived at Heathrow Airport, looking years younger than his acknowledged thirty-nine years, he asked me a question. 'What group or organization is behind all this. My manager wants to know. He worries about things like that.'

'What would he do if I tell him it's just us?' I wondered.

'Well...' I swallowed hard. 'The group is the Father, Son and Holy Ghost. The organization is an organism called the Body of Christ!' Pat smiled warmly, 'That suits me just fine.'

The concert tour began. Thousands of British people crowded the largest halls from Edinborough to London to share the musical experience of Come Together. After waiting for hours, they rushed for seats to hear the mass choir sing songs that became dear to their hearts and familiar in churches. The so-called reserved British responded with upraised hands in worship, stretching across seats to form prayer groups with strangers, and with tears answered God's call to serve.

It was as I had said to those who saw the film, 'What you see - the ardent worship, uplifted hands, tear-stained faces, joyful clapping, hugs among strangers and people huddled together in prayer - these are not American nor British reactions, but sincere responses to the Holy Spirit.'

Hundreds, in every city, for ten glorious days, responded, accepting the Savior. A spiritual awakening had begun. But it was only the start.

CHAPTER FIFTEEN

IN THE LAST DAYS

' A nd in the last days it shall be, God declares, that I will
pour out my Spirit upon all flesh, and your sons and
daughters will prophesy, and your young men shall see visions, and your old men shall dream dreams; yea, and on
my menservants and my maidservants in those days, I will
pour out my Spirit; and they shall prophesy. And I will show
wonders in the heaven above and signs in the earth beneath, Blood and fire and vapor of smoke; and the sun shall
be turned into darkness and the moon into blood, before
the day of the Lord comes, the great and manifest day. And
it shall be that whoever calls on the name of the Lord shall
be saved.' (Acts 2:17-21 RSV)

The Bible lay open upon my lap as I sat on the lanai.
The setting sun had stretched a brilliant scarf of color across
the sky, above the blue Pacific. Another day was ending in
Hawaii.

'The older I get, the faster the days seem to go by,' I
mused. 'There are not nearly enough left for me to do all

the things I would like to do before I meet the Lord. Yet, in some ways, I long for that day to come soon. I get a little home-sick for heaven, sometimes.'

Heaven! I recalled my mother's words,' Jean, heaven is not very far away...just a heart-beat away. It is another dimension.' I smiled as I thought of how real heaven was to all of us after her remarkable experience of dying and being restored to life by prayer.

'Why, that's incredible!' I suddenly realized my mother had been born twice, once as a baby and born again as a child of God. And she died twice! My mother had lived another thirty years before she went to heaven, again.

My father, several years later, went on to join her. La Donna Dalrymple, the evangelist, who led us to the Lord in the Toledo, Ohio, conducted Dad's funeral. She vividly recalled the night when we first came into the Foursquare Gospel church.

'As I remember it,' she said,' Mrs. Murphy, after noticing there were some black people in our congregation, was upset and wanted to go home. She had strong racial prejudice from her southern up-bringing.' LaDonna Dalrymple paused.

'However, I might add, her heart was later cleansed of that sin and afterwards, she and John were glad to host a black evangelist and his family in their home. Anyway, that night she was ready to leave. But her husband, John, placed his foot firmly against the end of the pew in front, blocking the exit to the aisle. He muttered, 'You drug us in here, but you're not dragging us out!' That remark, even at Dad's funeral, made us all smile!

LaDonna Dalrymple went on, 'John Murphy put one foot in heaven's door at that moment and opened the way for the whole family to come to Jesus. Now, he's stepped right inside, over the threshold. He is with his wonderful Lord. Once again he and his precious wife are united, never to part again.'

It seemed, for a moment, I could see them all; my parents, Elmer's parents and, yes, the evangelist herself, smiling from heaven.

As I glanced down at the Bible on my lap, opened to Acts 2:17-21, it seemed I could hear the evangelist's voice again, 'These are the last days. From the Day of Pentecost to the Day of the Lord, when Jesus comes again, are the last days of grace: This is the time for the sons and daughters of the last days to prophesy and see visions.'

Visions! It was the vision of a lost world without Jesus that caused me as say when I was fifteen years old, 'Oh Jesus, here's my life, add to it, or take from it what you will, only there is just one thing I ask, dear Lord. Please, when I have finished my life's work in your fields, let me meet you with my arms laden down with golden sheaves......'

I smiled as I realized how good the Lord has been to Elmer and to me. He granted us many years of service in Panama, the United States, Canada, Australia, Hong Kong and in Britain.

Twenty-five years in England! It was the vision of fires all over Britain, that kept us there. Fires of renewal that would blaze into revival.

'Feed the fires that I light,' the Lord had said. Elmer fed the fires when he founded Christian Life College at Post Green. Later, the college moved to London, where it continues today. I fed the fires as I ministered wherever God lighted his fires in Britain and Europe. During the last five years of our ministry in England, we formed a congregation, which became the nucleus for the First Foursquare Gospel Church in London.

I glanced again at the scripture in Acts, '...your sons and your daughters shall prophesy.'

Our son, John and our daughter, LaDonna grew up loving the Lord. They both married Christians and, with their families live for God.

John and his wife, Ruby, live in Hawaii. After several years with the College of Communications at the Kona Youth With A Mission base, John travels extensively, teaching Christian Communications. Their three children, Sharolyn, Johanna and Jonathan love the Lord and are seeking to do his will. Sharolyn, and her husband, Blake, blessed us with our first great-grandson, Cole.

Our daughter, LaDonna, married a Christian from Northern Ireland, Alan Elliott. They and their two sons, Ian and Matthew, live in London.

London! How difficult it was to leave, but the Lord had spoken to us. Only his voice could have caused us to leave the ones we loved so much. He asked us to turn our leadership over to others. It was obvious that God had Alan and La Donna ready to take on the pastorate of the church and to have a vital role in the continuation of Christian Life College. God also told us to move to Hawaii.

Moving to Hawaii was not a new idea to us. We thought of doing it five years earlier. At that time, we planned to go to a Crossroads DTS (Discipleship Training School) at the Youth With A Mission base in Kailua-Kona. The idea had developed after I had a heart attack in London.

I was at a March For Jesus rally in London at Kensington Temple. A sudden hot pain shot through my chest and held it with a grip. I thought it would never let go. The pain streaked out and down my arm from my chest. Gasping, weak and afraid, I moved with caution from the crowd and made my way down the stairs from the balcony. The pastor, Wyn Lewis, saw me and sensed something was wrong. He prayed for me. Strengthened, I drove home alone. When Elmer came home after teaching at the college, he didn't hesitate getting me to the Middlesex Hospital.

'Well, our tests show you're in need of heart surgery, probably a triple-bypass, Mrs. Darnall.' The doctor did not offer me any options, but I asked for one.

We had planned a trip to Hawaii to attend a training school, sort of a spiritual tune-up for Christian leaders,' I explained. The doctor didn't look too pleased.

'She won't be preaching,' Elmer added. 'The sessions are in the mornings only, so she can rest in the afternoons.'

After promising I would get plenty of rest, the doctor consented to our going to Kona. An appointment was made for when we returned to appraise the situation and to plan for an operation.

At first, the Kona climate, compared to the English weather, was a tonic. I felt so good I almost forgot there was anything wrong with my heart; but then the pain increased. Finally, I was unable to walk to the dining area, and my meals were served in our room.

One of our lecturers was Derek Prince. Elmer insisted that I make an effort to attend a divine healing service Derek and his wife, Ruth were to have in a local church. Although I was reluctant, I made the effort, for Elmer's sake. After Derek finished his powerful message on divine healing, many people went forward for prayer. So did we. Several couples from our Crossroads class were there. Derek said he and Ruth would pray for the couples from Crossroads first. I felt sorry for the rest of the sick people and a little embarrassed that we were chosen ahead of them. To our surprise, after he laid hands upon us and prayed, Derek instructed those who had received prayer to turn around and minister to all the rest of the people! Then Derek and Ruth left!

'I can't do this,' I thought. To lift my arms was an effort. After I prayed for several people, I realized I felt stronger. 'It must be the anointing,' I thought. 'I'll collapse when we get back to our room.' But instead, I found I could breathe easier than I had for months. The next morning I took a walk and attended class. I ate my meals in the dining pavilion.

It was then that I thought we should join the staff at Kona, but Elmer had other thoughts. 'I just can't do it Jean. I don't feel it is God's will for us to come here at this time. We must go back to London after Crossroads. There is more work for us to do.' I looked into his eyes and I knew he was right.

Back in London, the doctor at Middlesex Hospital was anxious to see me. He had expected to schedule a bypass operation. He set up appointments for more tests. After he studied the results, he said, 'Mrs. Darnall, Hawaii must have agreed with you. Your heart is in good condition. You won't need surgery. Whatever you are doing, keep it up!'

An island breeze picked up the pages of my Bible and, with invisible fingers, turned the pages. I put my hand on the Bible to hold the pages down. I laid my other hand upon my heart.

'Lord, thank you for healing me. I am so glad we returned to London. You did so much for us in those last four years. It was like setting our house on order, so that LaDonna and Alan, with others, could follow on an established path. Then, you called us here, to Hawaii. It seems an odd place for Elmer and me, out here on this piece of coral in the middle of the Pacific. Some people think we have come here to retire! Jesus, you know that can't be. In fact we've not retired, we've refired! Thank you Lord, for the strength to go all over the world for you with the anointing of the Holy Spirit. It is such a joy to be a part of these wonderful last days.

I looked down at the Bible, to the pages where the breezes had blown it open. The words spoke to me, 'I was not disobedient to the heavenly vision.'

'Remember how I gave you a vision for Britain?' the Lord asked.

'I'll never forget,' I whispered.

'Do you remember my answer when you asked me why I gave you that vision?' Acts 26:19

'You asked us to feed the fires that you lighted.' I sensed the nearness of the Lord. It seemed his smile, like sunshine, was all over me.

'My child, you were faithful to feed the fires in Britain. They are still burning and they will burn brighter. But I am lighting fires in many other nations in preparation for a worldwide spiritual awakening. The time is near when Revival fires I have lighted in many lands will explode and shake the world awake. The powerful sounds of the gospel of the kingdom will be like the roar of an erupting volcano. My child, I will increase your prophetic anointing for nations. Feed the fires I light wherever I send you.'

'That's why we're here Lord!'

Suddenly, I understood. Ever since we came to Hawaii, we have been going out from the island to the nations. There had been return trips to Australia and often to South Korea.

Korea! A nation, reached by missionaries less than three hundred years ago. But today the praying church in South Korea has a destiny to become God's newest missionary army.

. . . During a time of worship in a Korean church in Seoul, I had seen a vision of a huge cross, lying horizontal, descending and hovering over the border between North and South Korea. A demonic wall of huge warrior spirits formed a wall at the border. They stood in close formation, a fierce barrier facing South Korea. But the cross came down, down until it stopped above the heads of the demons. The top of the cross, above the crossbar, tilted downward towards the ground in North Korea, behind the enemy's lines. It pierced the earth and plunged underground. The cross was like a lever, one end underground in North Korea and the other end slanted and suspended above the people of South Korea. I observed a crowd of people gathered, standing, on the top of the lower end of the cross, a multitude of prayer warriors.

They prayed with intense energy. With faces lifted upward, arms extended, they jumped high and bounced up and down upon the end of the cross. Their prayers caused the upper end of the cross, inserted in the ground of North Korea to vibrate and to move the earth. At that moment, I noticed a commotion on the border at the top of North Korea. It caused the leaders to stare anxiously northward. They were so preoccupied they failed to notice how prayer was effecting North Korea, near the southern border.

The commotion at the top was not caused by soldiers, but by people dressed in business suits who carried briefcases. It was not a military disturbance but appeared to me like a commercial or business crisis. The problems there had the full attention of the North Korean leaders. Suddenly, as the South Koreans prayed with more fervor, the cross broke up through the ground behind the border. Thousands of God's people from South Korea flooded across and took the country with shouts of joy.

. . . It was night in Hawaii. The sky was studded with brilliant stars. A full moon came over the mountains. Awed by the stillness around me, I prayed, 'Lord, thank you for the vision you gave to me in Seoul. I stood and lifted my arms heavenward.

'Why, Lord, there must be more visions for more nations!'

The words came to me, '...on my handmaidens in those days I will pour my Spirit; and they shall prophesy...'

Somewhere, a new day was dawning I whispered, 'Heaven, here I come...but not yet!

For additional copies of

send $9.99 + $3.95 shipping and handling to:

WinePress Publishing
PO Box 1406
Mukilteo, WA 98275

or have your credit card ready and call:

(800) 917-BOOK